"An excellent new book—as fresh as an ocean breeze. It will bring a new generation of hikers back to the forgotten trails of the Coast Range and Siskiyous."

——Tony George, Author, *The Mount Jefferson Wilderness Guidebook;* member, Chemeketans Hiking Club, Salem

"This informative and readable trail guide should encourage hikers to explore the mountains along Oregon's coastline."

——Tom L. Thompson, Forest Supervisor/Siuslaw National Forest

"It's time the hiking trails on the west side of the I-5 corridor got some attention. This is the first book I'm aware of that provides extensive coverage of this area. Careless land-use practices have ravaged many of Oregon's coastal mountains, but this book is an invitation to explore the beautiful spots that remain. It is also a reminder to hikers of the value of participation in land-use decisions."

——Bob Wilson, Business Manager Portland Chapter, Audubon Society

"If ever there was a justification for guidebooks to the backcountry, it is to save wild areas from ruthless exploitation. The most effective conservation lobbyists are those who've come to know a wild and beautiful place from days of hiking, nights of camping. This book should do wonders for Oregon's beleaguered forests."

——Jon Harlin, Associate Editor, *BACKPACKER* Magazine; author, *The Climber's Guide to North America*

"*50 Hikes* provides very useful insight to some beautiful areas that are not often visited."

——Ron Pugh, Trail Coordinator Siskiyou National Forest

50 Hikes in Oregon's COAST RANGE & SISKIYOUS

Rhonda and George Ostertag

The Mountaineers • Seattle

The Mountaineers: Organized 1906 "... to explore, study, preserve, and enjoy the natural beauty of the Northwest."

3 2 1 0 9
5 4 3 2 1

Published by The Mountaineers
306 Second Avenue West, Seattle, Washington 98119

Published simultaneously in Canada by Douglas & McIntyre, Ltd., 1615 Venables Street, Vancouver, B.C. V5L 2H1

Manufactured in the United States of America

Edited by Heath Silberfeld
Cover design by Nick Gregoric
Layout by Nick Gregoric
Cover photograph: Western azaleas along the trail near Doe Gap, Kalmiopsis Wilderness, Hike 47
Frontispiece: Nancy Creek, Hike 41
Maps by Rhonda Ostertag
Photos by George Ostertag

Library of Congress Cataloging-in-Publication Data

Ostertag, Rhonda, 1957–
50 hikes in Oregon's Coast Range and Siskiyous / Rhonda and George Ostertag.
p. cm.
Includes index.
ISBN 0-89886-200-0
1. Hiking—Oregon—Guide-books. 2. Oregon—Description and travel—1981– —Guide-books. I. Ostertag, George, 1957– II. Title. III. Title: Fifty hikes in Oregon's Coast Range and Siskiyous.
GV199.42.07084 1989
917.95—dc19

89-3150
CIP

CONTENTS

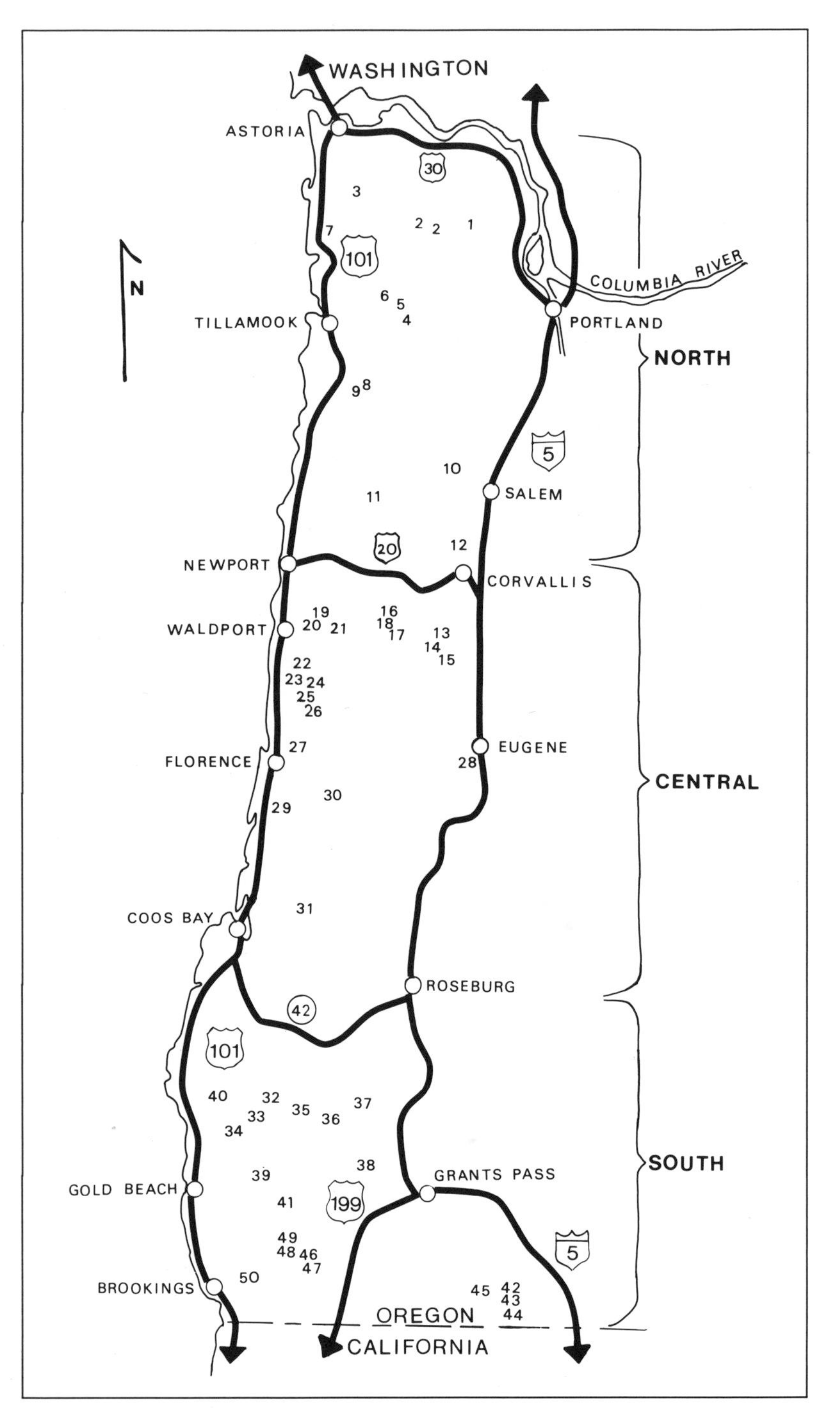
WASHINGTON
ASTORIA
30
3
2
2
1
7
101
N
COLUMBIA RIVER
6
5
4
TILLAMOOK
PORTLAND
NORTH
9
8
5
10
11
SALEM
20
12
NEWPORT
CORVALLIS
19
16
WALDPORT
20
21
18
17
13
14
15
22
23
24
25
26
27
EUGENE
FLORENCE
28
CENTRAL
30
29
31
COOS BAY
ROSEBURG
42
101
40
32
35
37
33
36
34
38
GRANTS PASS
SOUTH
39
GOLD BEACH
41
199
49
48
46
47
5
BROOKINGS
50
45
42
43
OREGON
44
CALIFORNIA

SOUTH TRAILS (South of Oregon 42) **Page**

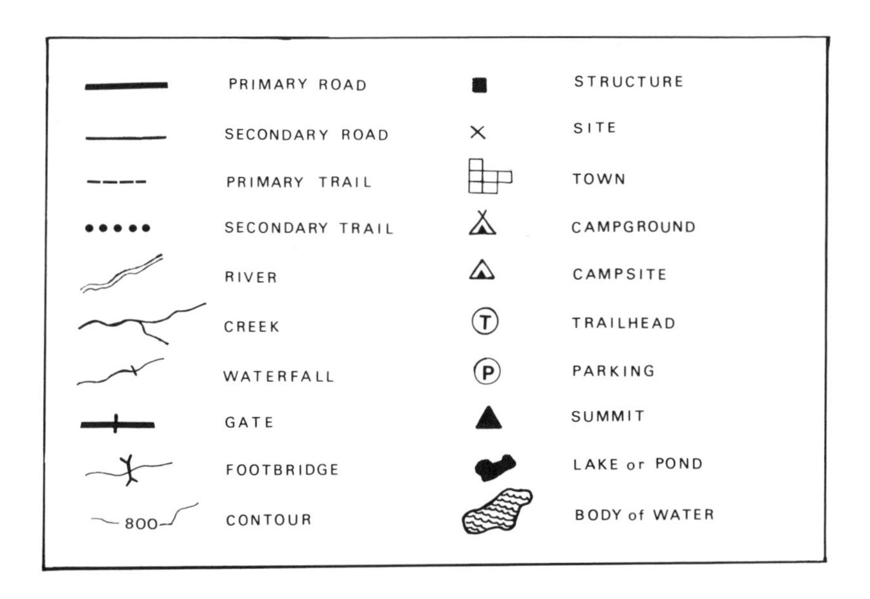

SAFETY CONSIDERATIONS

Travel in many parts of the backcountry entails unavoidable risks that every traveler assumes and must be aware of and respect. The fact that an area is described in this book is not a representation that it will be safe for you. Trips vary greatly in difficulty and in the amount and kind of preparation needed to enjoy them safely. Some routes may have changed, or conditions on them may have deteriorated since this book was written. Also, of course, conditions can change even from day to day, owing to weather and other factors. A trip that is safe in good weather or for a highly conditioned, properly equipped traveler may be completely unsafe for someone else or unsafe under adverse weather conditions.

You can minimize your risks by being knowledgeable, prepared, and alert. There is not space in this book for a general treatise on wilderness safety, but there are a number of good books and public courses on the subject, and you should take advantage of them to increase your knowledge. Just as important, you should always be aware of your own limitations and conditions existing when and where you are traveling. If conditions are dangerous, or if you are not prepared to deal with them safely, change your plans! It is better to have wasted a few days than to be the subject of a wilderness rescue. These warnings are not intended to keep you out of the backcountry. Many people enjoy safe trips through the backcountry every year. However, one element of the beauty, freedom, and excitement of the wilderness is the presence of risks that do not confront us at home. When you travel in the backcountry, you assume those risks. They can be met safely, but only if you exercise your own independent judgment and common sense.

The Mountaineers

PREFACE

George and I had long wanted to pair our writing/photography enterprise with our favorite avocation—hiking—but the timing or the subject was never quite right. With our move to Oregon, the concept of writing a trail guide finally reached maturity. What better way to become acquainted with our new home? The timing was certainly right, and the outdoor enthusiast couldn't hope for better subject matter than that found in Oregon.

It was Oregon's coastal mountain corridor that, in the end, attracted us. These mountains sparked our curiosity because of the absence of information on their recreation potential. But the area completely won us over when we put boot rubber to our research.

Despite extensive logging, Oregon's Coast Range and Siskiyou Mountains house caches of wilderness splendor that any hiker would want to explore and preserve. Now that we've kicked down the information barrier, we take this opportunity to invite the reader to sample firsthand the offerings of Oregon's coastal mountains.

POLITICS AND THE HIKER

For many hikers, the coupling of politics with the joy of a wilderness experience is incongruous. Politics is an involved process, sometimes disintegrating into a seedy piece of business, while hiking rejoices in a purer state—focusing on communion with nature, introspection, and a retreat from the tensions and congestion of the workday world. But more and more, it is becoming apparent that hikers must create a political voice to ensure the preservation of their prized retreats.

The Coast Range is an outstanding example of the dangers of hiker silence. For years the public lands in this range have been abandoned to the whim of the chain saw. The result has been the loss of trails through neglect, through upgrading of trails to road status, and through complete clearing of land.

Similar threat now befalls the Siskiyou Mountain trails.

We don't wish to yell down the timber industry. It has long played a role in Oregon history and will always hold a place in Oregon's economy. What we would like to challenge is the lumbering activity that is occurring on our public lands—our multiple-use lands—to the exclusion of other activities and other party interests.

No longer can the dollar value of board feet be held paramount. The costs, too, must be addressed: the cost to fisheries and to watersheds, and the cost to wildlife and recreation. Then, there's the intrinsic value of forest habitat that supersedes economic consideration.

The impact of timbering-fouled waterways is only now receiving its deserved attention with a push for greater easements along streambeds and the saving of timber-valued trees within those easements.

With such precious little wilderness remaining, it's important that the actions of our public land stewards not go uncensored. Mining, grazing, and timbering activities carry too great a cost. An error in judgment today may cost us the wilderness of tomorrow.

As hikers, and as the "public," we should all take the time to review how our public lands are being managed and comment on it. The trailhead registry offers an accessible hiker forum. Critical comments count, and in number they can bring about change.

ABOUT TRAIL PURITY

Trail purity—that is, single-use trails—is a cause all hikers can rally behind. Save for the trails that are closed to motorized vehicles in our National Park System and Wilderness Areas, an alarming number of trails are falling under a classification of shared-use for hikers and off-road-vehicle (ORV) enthusiasts. And with the organized political voice of the latter group, this trend is likely to continue, robbing hikers of the wilderness experience.

ORV groups complain that it is a matter of rights. Indeed it is a matter of rights. A hiker poses little threat to the ORV experience, save as an obstacle for which the driver must slow. Conversely, an off-road vehicle deprives the hiker of the tranquil pursuit of nature. Roaring engines, exhaust fumes, tread marks instead of animal tracks, crushed vegetation, eroding trails, and the absence of wildlife do not reward the physical expenditure or fulfill the spirit. Moreover, there is a question of hiker safety when trails are open for joint use.

ORV groups complain that they should have equal access to the vistas and attractions afforded to hikers. Agreed. ORV enthusiasts should have equal access to these natural splendors. Their motorized vehicles should not.

These pristine treasures exist largely due to their isolation. Rightly, they should be reserved only for those willing to expend the effort to secure an audience. The preservation of these treasures demands this limited-access management.

With the divergent orientations of these two groups, it is a farce to consider addressing the interests of both with a single-trail system. To the ORV enthusiast, a trail is an access. To the hiker, the trail introduces an encounter with nature.

As hikers, we must push for the halt of joint-use trail programs. A separate system serving the needs of each group and meeting the overriding needs of nature must be sought.

ACKNOWLEDGMENTS

We would like to acknowledge the many people who helped bring this book to its conclusion, beginning with the staff at The Mountaineers Books for their patient guidance. For their kind attention to the many phone inquiries and their attentive reading of the trail drafts, we also thank the personnel at the following agencies: Siuslaw National Forest, Siskiyou National Forest, Oregon State Parks and Recreation Division, Oregon State Department of Forestry, Oregon State Department of Fish and Wildlife, the Bureau of Land Management, Oregon Caves National Monument, the Willamette Valley national wildlife refuges, the Oregon State University College of Forestry, and the City of Eugene Parks Planning and Development. Lastly, we thank the people we met along the trail who lent their faces and impressions to this book.

Rhonda and George Ostertag

Pitcher plant in the Kalmiopsis wilderness

INTRODUCTION

Together, the Siskiyou Mountains and the Coast Range compose Oregon's coastal mountains, and together they represent an untapped recreation wonderland.

Yet there is but peripheral mention of Coast Range trails in a few guidebooks, and general guides to Oregon barely mention this range, save as the dividing landmark between the Oregon Coast and the Willamette Valley.

Even the telephone information disseminated by the various management agencies either downplays the hiking opportunities in this region or promotes the hiking elsewhere in Oregon.

But the Coast Range has a lot to offer. We discovered caches of beautiful old-growth forests, record-sized trees, towering waterfalls, ocean and valley vistas, scenic creeks and rivers, and some superb trails.

The attractions were there. What wasn't there were current maps and a general feeling among the public agencies that Oregon's Coast Range is more than just a "timber factory"—that it is also a recreation land.

Propagating the myth of inaccessibility is the checkerboard ownership of the Coast Range and its foothills. State, private, and federal parties hold stewardship to this land in interlocking, sometimes small, tracts.

For multiple-use management areas, it is this structuring of the land that has become the excuse for the absence of trails (a "soft" land-use practice) and the vindication for current "exploitive" practices. A casual perusal of a map, however, reveals that even where the land ownership is checkerboard, single-ownership tracts of suitable size for trails do exist, and even small tracts can support nature trails.

The theory prevails, however, with an impact hard felt. In its Salem, Eugene, and Coos Bay districts, the Bureau of Land Management holds hundreds of thousands of acres west of Interstate 5 and east of U.S. 101, yet together, these three districts offer but 1.2 miles of trail. True, much of that area is ex-railroad land not falling under the Federal Land Policy and Management Act (FLPMA), but 1.2 miles of trail is a sorry statement for this expanse.

Elliott State Forest, which is promoted as a multiple-use area, offers no developed trails and has abandoned the maintenance of its School Land Bay Nature Trail.

Despite this grim report, all is not dark. Change is on the horizon. At Tillamook State Forest, a committed volunteer trail staff is gradually upgrading the trail system, minimizing the sections of joint-use trail (trail open to off-road-vehicle riders and hikers). And as the new State Forestry Board holds a broader interpretation of forest management than that held in the past, the door remains open for recreation and further trail-enhancement efforts.

Likewise, the coastal mountain trail system managed by the National Forest Service is approaching full cycle, with the reclamation of former roads for trails, the reopening of many neglected trails, and ambitious long-range plans for expanding and interconnecting major trails. Trails reclaimed from roads have already added to the Cape Perpetua system and have provided access to Grassy Knob and Cummins Creek wildernesses.

Much of this awakened interest in trail development and maintenance can be traced to a change in forest management philosophy. Previously, trails were the jurisdiction of transportation management. Today they are properly reclassified under recreation and are considered to have merit for their own sake, making funding more readily available.

Indeed Oregon's coastal mountains represent a burgeoning recreation area, and the trail system, now in a second infancy, invites the hiker to explore and to sample the promise of the future.

With this book, we hope to supply the reader with the directions and information necessary to conduct those explorations. We also hope to stimulate an interest in Oregon's coastal mountains that will encourage both their protection and their continued promotion as recreation lands.

USE OF THE BOOK

We have selected a complement of hikes in the area west of Interstate 5 and east of U.S. 101, north of California and south of the Columbia River. The wealth of this Oregon corridor includes three national forests, four state forests, four wild and scenic rivers, seven wilderness areas, four wildlife refuges, a national monument, and a smattering of state parks.

In this book, the reader will find nature trails, day hikes, car shuttles, and backpacks. We believe there are hikes to appeal to all interests and capabilities and that we have provided the information necessary for the reader to identify the hikes best suited to individual preferences and energies.

We've tried to structure the book to aid in selecting trails. First, the trails are grouped by region: north, central, and south, with U.S. 20 and Oregon 42 dividing the region into thirds. Second, to discover the character of a trail at a glance, each trail write-up

Rhododendron blooms invite a closer appreciation.

begins with a summary table identifying trail length, elevation change, and degree of difficulty.

The individual write-ups introduce the natural history of the area, deliver detailed directions to the trailhead, and describe the progress of the trail, drawing attention to special features and alerting the hiker to obstacles and potentially confusing junctions.

Road building and lumbering activity in the coastal mountains necessitate the detail of the directions, as the maps for this area rapidly become dated. Using a write-up in conjunction with a forest-service map is the best bet for a no-fuss delivery to the trailhead.

For use of the summary table, an explanation of terms is in order to avoid any misinterpretation. Distance measures represent pedometer readings of round-trip distance, with the exception of the one-way car shuttles that are clearly specified. For the most part, backpacking excursions—sometimes dictated by distance, sometimes by attraction—are left to the hiker's own judgment. The elevation change is the difference between elevation extremes.

The classification of trail difficulty as easy, moderate, or strenuous is subjective. Easy hikes are generally short (under 3 miles) and have an elevation change of less than 500 feet. Moderate hikes usually fall within the distance range of 3 to 7 miles and carry a maximum elevation change of 1000 feet, and strenuous hikes are all those with a distance exceeding 7 miles and carrying an elevation change greater than 1000 feet. Considerations that may override these fundamental guidelines are trail condition and grade, obstacles, and, to a lesser degree, exposure to the elements.

Matching the hike to the willingness and ability of the hiking party lays the foundation for an enjoyable trip.

HIKING HINTS

Many hikers return from their excursions pleasantly exhausted, but with spirit refreshed and full of praise for the adventure. Others return footsore, dehydrated, and irritable. Hiking is not for everyone. But often the poor wilderness experience can be traced back to the degree of preparation.

To enjoy nature's beauty, sometimes the hiker must experience a little discomfort: sun, insects, steep terrain, brush. But the prepared hiker learns to anticipate such evils and takes measures to eliminate or minimize their effects. Learning and heeding the regulations for backcountry use, becoming familiar with the area and its maps, and properly equipping for the demands of the trail and the climatic conditions will smooth the way to a friendly encounter with nature.

Preparation

Attending to these Ten Essentials provides a head start to a safe and rewarding outdoor adventure:

1. Extra Clothing—more than is needed in good weather
2. Extra Food—so that something is left over at the end of the trip
3. Sunglasses—especially important for alpine and snow travel
4. Knife—for first aid and emergency fire building (making kindling)

5. Firestarter—a candle or chemical fuel for starting a fire with wet wood
6. First-aid Kit—the hiker should also have basic first-aid knowledge, with CPR skills a plus
7. Matches—in a waterproof container
8. Flashlight—with extra bulb and batteries
9. Map—the right one for the trip
10. Compass—with knowledge of how to use it and the declination

Clothing. The amount and types of clothing worn and carried on a hike depend on the length of the outing, weather conditions, and individual comfort requirements. Generally speaking, though, layering is the code word. Wool is the fabric of choice for cold, wet, or changeable weather. It serves the hiker much as it did its original owner, retaining heat even when wet. Cotton is the fabric of warm summer days.

Hats are lightweight articles of clothing that provide a major service. In the summer, they shield the eyes, face, and top of the head from the sun. In winter, they preserve body heat.

In Oregon, one necessity is a good suit of rain gear—jacket or poncho, with pants or chaps. Except in midsummer, the unexpected rainstorm should always be expected. Most hikers agree: The comfort provided during a major cloudburst easily compensates for the added weight on those other excursions where the raingear went unused.

On a day hike, a large plastic garbage bag can often pinch-hit. It's lightweight, compact, and water resistant.

Footgear. "Tennies" are appropriate for short hikes on soft earthen trails, if conditions are dry. For long hikes and hikes on uneven terrain, boots are preferred for both comfort and protection. While the light weight of sneakers may be appealing, after a long day on the trail that appeal departs as the feet carry the aching memory of each and every pebble encounter.

Sock layering, with a light undersock worn next to the foot and a wool sock worn atop, helps to prevent rubbing and allows for the absorption of perspiration.

Food. The guideline for food is to pack plenty. Hiking demands a lot of energy. Whenever possible, strive to maximize the energy value of the food for its weight, particularly for backpacking. With Oregon's wet weather, it's also a good idea to choose foods in moisture-resistant wrappers. Cardboard and paper do not fare well in the rain.

Food helps fend off fatigue, a major contributor to accidents on the trail.

Equipment. The quantity and variety of equipment carried in addition to the Ten Essentials depends on the length and nature of the hike and the season. But a good pack for transporting that gear is essential. Generally, a day pack with padded straps, a reinforced bottom, and side pockets for water bottles is appropriate for the short outing. For backpacking, it's important to select a pack that carries the weight without taxing the hips and shoulders or creating a strain on the neck.

As backpacks represent a major investment, we recommend the newcomer to the sport try renting one first. It's difficult to evaluate a pack in a store with only a few sandbags for weight. A trail test delivers a better comfort reading, plus it demonstrates how well the unit packs with one's personal gear. Moreover, most good backpacking stores with a rental program deduct the cost of one rental from the purchase price of a pack.

Camera equipment, binoculars, and nature guides are optional gear that may enhance a trip for the hiker.

Map and Compass. Taking the time to become familiar with maps and with map reading in conjunction with a compass will only increase one's enjoyment of the outdoors, and it may open up a whole new world of adventure. Maps are important tools. They provide orientation to an area, suggest alternate routes, present new areas to explore, and aid in planning and preparation for the journey.

Different types of maps supply different information:

1. United States Forest Service (USFS) maps provide a wealth of information. They show the roads and road surfaces, the maintained trails (at the time of the map making), land ownership, campgrounds, waterways, and major landmarks. What these maps do not show is the topography of the land.

They are a good single source for gaining an overall picture of the area, but they provide limited information about the character of the trail.

Forest Service maps are available at the Ranger District offices, Forest Service headquarters, and outdoors shops.

2. Topographic maps (topos) are necessary for any cross-country excursion and prove a valuable aid for reading the progress of the trail. Topos show elevations, suggest the terrain, show primary and secondary trails, indicate groundcover, show watercourses, and indicate the works of man. The United States Geological Survey offers topos in two sizes: the 7.5-minute series and the 15-minute series.

The drawback with the maps for the coastal mountains is that they are outdated. The area is dynamic. Trails have been abandoned, new trails have been added, and old trails have been ex-

Upper Coquille River Falls, Hike 35

tended, but these maps continue to deliver useful information about the terrain.

Topos are available at most outdoor and mountaineering/ski shops or by writing to the USGS, Western District Center, Federal Center, Denver, CO 80225.

As a reminder, for proper reading of these maps a magnetic declination of the compass is necessary, as true north does not equal magnetic north. For Oregon, the mean declination is 20 degrees east. For specific locales, the declination may vary one to two degrees. Most topos indicate the declination on the bottom border of the map.

Taking to the Trails

Pace. Adopting a steady rhythm or pace will allow greater comfort in logging distances. Maintaining this rhythm with an adjustment for stride also facilitates a climb.

Psychology comes into play on the hills. If the eyes are forever trained on the top of the hill and the steps are belabored, all one can sense are those straining calf and thigh muscles, and the discomfort of the climb becomes amplified. Conversely, if one allows the eyes to play on the surroundings, maintains a steady hiking pace, and perhaps even strikes up a conversation, the time on the hill passes more quickly and the physical taxation is deemphasized.

A measured pace along with short rests at moderate intervals guards against over-exhaustion.

Stream crossings. When stream conditions make dry crossing impossible, it's best to cross at the widest part of the watercourse, where the current is slower and the water more shallow. Sandy bottoms suggest a barefoot crossing, while fast, cold waters and rocky bottoms require a surer footing, calling for removal of socks and wading in one's boots. When sock-covered feet are returned to wet boots, the wool content of the socks will keep the feet warm. Rag socks with high cotton content should be avoided. They have poorer heat retention, and once wet are slow to dry.

Hiking in wet boots may be uncomfortable, but it's a minor discomfort compared to the alternative dunking.

Cross-country. Cross-country excursions, save for short distances, are not for beginners. To safely travel cross-country, one must have good map, compass, and wilderness skills, and good common sense.

In Oregon's coastal mountains, cross-country hiking opportunities are limited. The thick evergreen forests that dominate this region deny the hiker visible landmarks by which to navigate, and the forest sameness introduces confusion. Add to this the steep terrain, heavy brush, and many downfalls that physically and mentally tax the hiker and you will know why cross-country explorations in this region are reserved for the few.

With the added energy expenditure involved in cross-country hiking, the potential for injury increases. Of all hiking, this type should not be attempted alone. Even know-how and preparation cannot fully arm one against the unpredictability of nature and the fallibility of man.

Wilderness Courtesy

Trails. Good hikers avoid shortcutting trails and enlarging the trail bed. Skirting puddles, walking two abreast, or walking along the bench of a recessed trail causes damage. Any damage to trails or signs should be reported to the managing agency.

Camping. With more and more people discovering the out-

Deer near Whiskey Creek, Hike 38

doors, low-impact camping should be the goal of every hiker. Wherever possible, hikers should select an established campsite and not rearrange it by removing groundcover, bringing in logs for benches, or digging drainage channels around tents. The clues that a hiker passed by should be minimal.

Campfires can be avoided with a backpacker's stove for cooking. When a campfire is necessary, it should be kept small, and regulations on campfires and wood gathering heeded.

If there are no pre-established campsites, a site well-removed from the water and from the trail is best. Delicate meadow environments should be avoided. The foot traffic alone, in and to the camp, can cause severe damage, scarring such areas for years to come.

Courtesy is also important when it comes to site selection. While locating a camp on an overlook or beside a special trail feature may prove tempting, the camp and its legacy will deprive others of an appreciation for that same view or offering.

Sanitation. For human waste disposal, a site well away from the trail and at least 300 feet from any watercourse is required, with a hole 6 to 8 inches deep for disposal and burying of waste. This biologically active layer of the soil holds organisms that can quickly decompose organic matter.

Tissue poses a greater problem, particularly in drier regions. If fire poses no danger, touching a match to the tissue will prevent its becoming nest-building material for a rodent or garbage scattered by salt-seeking deer. Where fire is a danger, leaves should be used in place of tissue.

If the ground prohibits digging a hole of the specified size, it should be dug as deep as possible and covered well with gravel, bark, and leaves.

Litter. "Pack it in, pack it out" is the rule. Any litter that does not completely burn should be carried out. This includes aluminum foil, cans, and the like.

Despite popular belief, orange peels, too, are garbage. It takes years for nature to reclaim an orange peel, and animals do not eat them.

Burying garbage is not a solution. Animals may still be attracted to the smell, which means torn up vegetation and garbage spread to the winds. Too, the metals in containers can contaminate the soil.

Cigarette butts should be taken apart and the paper and filter packed out for proper disposal. Gum chewers should pocket the wrappers and package pull-strings.

Washing. Washing of body or dishes should be done well away from lakes or streams. Water should be carried to the washing site and biodegradable soap used sparingly. Despite their many benefits and their ecological-sounding name, biodegradable soaps still present a threat to water. Whenever possible, select a rocky wash site, removed from vegetation.

Noise. Nature's quiet and the privacy of fellow hikers deserve respect. The hiker is a guest in the wild and should use guestlike manners.

Safety

Each hiker brings to the trail a different set of skills and abilities, skills and abilities that can change with time. Independent judgment and common sense remain a hiker's best allies.

When traveling in the backcountry, hikers assume the risk but also reap the rewards.

Water. Water is the preferred refreshment. Drinks with caffeine or alcohol are diuretics and serve to dehydrate and weaken the hiker.

Carrying one's drinking water in ample quantity promises a safe drinking supply. Water from trail sources must be properly treated before drinking. Today, few streams are self-purifying. Pollution, *Giardia,* and other evils lurk within the clear waters.

Boiling the water for ten minutes still provides the best protection, although it is an admittedly tedious task. Some of the new water filtration systems offer a relatively safe alternative, but these filters come in varying degrees of sophistication. The system selected must strain out harmful organisms and debris. Iodine tablets offer less protection and no protection against *Giardia.* They are not considered safe for pregnant women.

It is best to carry some water on all excursions. Sources can dry up or become fouled. Even on short nature hikes, water is a good companion. If thirsty, one can't enjoy the trail's offerings.

Getting Lost. Before venturing out on any hike, word should be left with someone about the planned destination and time of return. Upon return, the informed party should be notified.

If lost, it's best to sit down and try to think calmly. There's no immediate danger, as long as one has packed properly and followed the notification procedure. If hiking with a group, all should stay together.

Conducting short outward searches for the trail and returning to a marked location if unsuccessful are generally safe. Aimless wandering would be a mistake.

If a search meets with failure, shouting or whistling in sets of three may bring help. (Combinations of three are universally recognized as distress signals.) If it's getting late in the day, the time is best used to prepare for night. Conserving energy is equally important.

Normally, unless one has good cross-country navigational

skills, efforts are better spent conserving energy and aiding the rescuers (by staying put, hanging out bright-colored clothing, and calling out or whistling) than by trying to walk to safety.

In Oregon's coastal mountains, however, with the riddling of roads and many watercourses to the ocean, the likelihood of becoming hopelessly lost is remote. But should one suffer an injury or otherwise become stranded, knowing proper procedure is a comfort.

Hypothermia. Hypothermia is the dramatic cooling of the body that occurs when heat loss surpasses body-heat generation.

Cold, wet, and windy weather demand respect. Attending to the Ten Essentials, eating properly, avoiding fatigue, and being alert to symptoms of sluggishness, clumsiness, and incoherence among hiking party members remain the best protection. The unpredictability of weather must always be respected.

Should a party member display symptoms of hypothermia, it is paramount to stop and get him or her dry and warm. Hot fluids are further recommended to help restore body heat.

Heat Exhaustion. The strenuous exercise of hiking combined with summer sun can lead to heat exhaustion, an overtaxation of the body's heat regulatory system. Wearing a hat, drinking plenty of water, eating properly (including salty snacks), and avoiding fatigue are the safeguards against heat exhaustion.

For those who are sensitive to the sun, hiking in the early morning and evening hours with midday rests proves beneficial. Wearing wet bandanas about the temples and neck and wet wrist bands introduces coolness to the pulse points, further minimizing the impact of heat and sun.

Poison Oak. The best guard against this demon is to know what the plant looks like and in what environments it commonly grows. A good plant identification book will supply this information.

Should one come in contact with the plant, an immediate rinse is advised.

The infected area should not be scratched or in any way covered. Heat also should be avoided. Any one of these will cause spreading. Exposure to air and time are still the best medicines. Scientists, however, are edging closer to the development of preventive weapons—creams or vaccines that will inhibit or reduce the effectiveness of the plant's poison.

Stings and Bites. It is a good idea for hikers to learn if they are allergic to bee stings before they enter the wilderness. Becoming versed in the habits and nature of these creatures and exercising caution when traveling cross-country help avoid stings and snake bites.

Hanging Rock, Hike 36

Bears. In dealing with bears, it's basic common sense. Food should not be stored near camp, and especially not in the tent. If clothes pick up cooking smells, it helps to suspend them from an overhanging branch well away from camp, along with the food. Sweet-smelling creams or lotions may prove enticing to a bear, too.

Trailhead Precautions. Hikers are a vulnerable lot. Their vehicles (and frequently their valuables) are left unattended for long periods of time in remote trailhead parking areas—a virtual invitation to the trailhead thief.

As a safeguard, while partaking in the wilderness experience, the following precautions should be heeded:

1. Whenever possible, do not park at the trailhead. Instead, park down the road or leave the car at a nearby campground or other facility. A car in the trailhead parking area says "my owner is gone."
2. Don't leave valuables. Carry keys and wallet, placing them in a remote compartment in the pack where they won't be disturbed until the return.
3. Do not leave any visible invitations to a thief. Whenever possible, stash everything in the trunk. If that's not possible, be sure any exposed item advertises that it has no value.
4. Be suspicious of anyone loitering at the trailhead. Some thieves have become quite creative. With a pack in tow, they sit at the trailhead parking area, presumably waiting for a ride. This allows them to easily observe gear unloading, the stashing of items in the trunk, and the hiding of valuables. It also allows them to naturally engage hikers in conversation, learning where they are going and when they'll return.

It's easier than taking candy from babies. The hiker won't squeal, until the return to the vehicle.

1 BANKS TO VERNONIA RAILROAD GRADE

Distance: 21 miles, walkable though unmaintained (one-way distance, fragmented by trestles and roads)
Elevation Change: 600 feet
Difficulty: Moderate
Maps: USGS Vernonia, Forest Grove
Water: Carry water
Season: All year
For More Information: State Parks Division, Salem

In 1975, with the idea of creating Oregon's first linear park, the State Parks Division paid $200,000 for the 21-mile stretch of Burlington Northern Railroad running between Banks and Vernonia. Across the nation, states have similarly reclaimed rails for trails with great success and public favor.

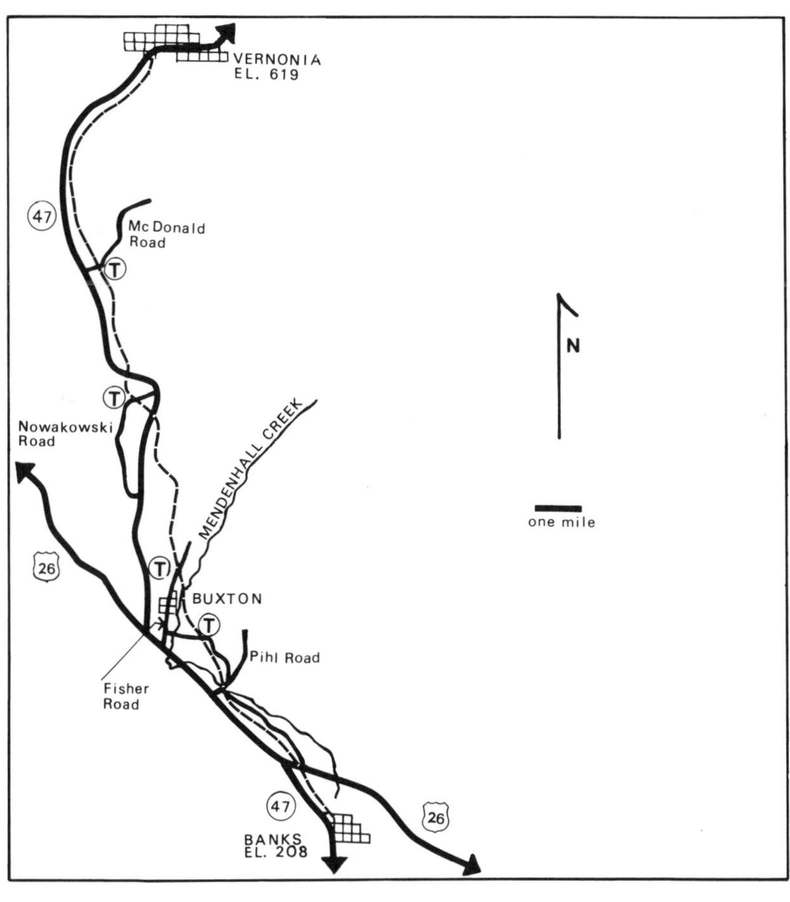

But the proposed use of this right-of-way has met with neighborhood opposition and funding limitations. The resulting years of limbo, together with the damage from clearcut slides and the fire of 1987, at times, have clouded the outlook for the trail's realization.

Still, the State Parks Division study findings confirm the recreational merit of this land strip, and in the fall of 1988, the Transportation Commission voted unanimously to pursue the park's development. The future of the trail now rests with the legislature, for endorsement and funding.

Meanwhile, the right-of-way, in its undeveloped state, is open to hikers. With widths of 60 to 1100 feet, the former railroad bed provides a relaxing corridor by which to tour the rural countryside. Much of the trail is time-healed and shaded by alders. With the rails and ties removed, the trail generally offers comfortable walking for all ages and abilities. A few areas retain a rocky surface.

The following segments provide a sampling of the railroad grade's potential:

The Buxton Trailheads: From Highway 26, go north on Fisher Road toward Buxton, bearing right onto Bacona Road in .7 mile. After another .6 mile, the trailhead lies at the end of the pavement. The westward-bound trail continues 3.4 miles to Oregon 47.

For a shorter trail from U.S. 26, go north on Fisher Road .4 mile and turn right onto Pongratz Road (a gravel road). The trailhead is on the left in .8 mile. In 1.3 miles, the trail concludes at the trestle over Mendenhall Creek.

Nowakowski Road Trailhead: From U.S. 26, take Oregon 47 north 5.1 miles, turning left onto Nowakowski Road. The trailhead is in .5 mile. Heading south, the trail concludes at Oregon 47 in .3 mile. Heading north, it concludes at Oregon 47 in 1.3 miles.

McDonald Road Trailhead: From U.S. 26, take Oregon 47 north 8.7 miles, turning right onto McDonald Road. The trailhead is in .1 mile. The trail continues south 2.9 miles to Oregon 47 or north 1.2 miles, before it becomes too overgrown for easy passage.

Since there are no formal parking areas, hikers should show consideration for private lands, drives and mailboxes. Too, in light of neighborhood sentiment, hikers should put on their best trail manners: respecting private property, packing it in/packing it out, and being their neighbor's keeper by policing the trail for litter or abuse. With so few trails in northwestern Oregon, hikers can ill afford to lose this one.

Alder and second-growth Douglas fir frame much of the trail, with trillium, Oregon grape, sword fern, salal, and blackberry contributing to the undergrowth. Clearcut parcels and meadow-

Trestle, Banks-Vernonia Railroad Grade

land alternate command of the trail with the second-growth forest. Openings offer views of the rural setting, the Coast Range foothills, and scenic creeks.

While there are occasional traffic sounds as the trail segments approach the main roads, much of the trail is secluded from such intrusions. The trail itself is closed to motorized vehicles.

For hiking, this one-time railroad grade holds no confusing junctions. But be alert to the danger presented by the major trestles, which were not designed for foot traffic. Although the trestles are closed to trail use, some of the warning signs are missing. When the park receives legislative endorsement and funding the trestles will be made safe for walkers.

Deer, rabbits, and grouse deliver unexpected entertainment along the trail.

2 4-COUNTY POINT AND SUNSET WAYSIDE

4-COUNTY POINT TRAIL

Distance: 1.5 miles round trip
Elevation Change: Insignificant
Difficulty: Easy
Map: Unnecessary
Water: Wolf Creek
Season: All year
For More Information: Oregon State Department of Forestry, Salem

SUNSET WAYSIDE TRAIL

Distance: 1.4-mile loop, nature trail
Elevation Change: 100 feet
Difficulty: Easy
Map: Unnecessary
Water: South Fork Rock Creek
Season: All year
For More Information: Oregon State Department of Forestry, Salem

The 4-County Point Trail takes the hiker on a leisurely stroll along the west bank of Wolf Creek, before winding to the commemorative marker denoting the only location in Oregon where four counties converge. Despite its proximity to the road, the trail pleases with its second-growth Douglas fir, sword fern, and Oregon grape. A gurgling Wolf Creek, moss-covered logs, and elk track on the trail add to the charm.

The Sunset Wayside Nature Trail provides a good introduction to the Coast Range and to the history of early logging. Touring this second-growth forest, the visitor learns to detect how trees were felled and transported, while gathering clues to the recent past of this forest. Again, there is some road noise.

U.S. 26 provides access to both of these trails. The 4-County Point Trail lies 2.9 miles west of the Timber turnoff on the north side of U.S. 26, just west of the Wolf Creek bridge. A green-and-white hiker sign indicates the trail.

Bridge over South Fork Rock Creek, Sunset Wayside Nature Trail

The Sunset Wayside Nature Trail is located 5.8 miles west of the 4-County Point trailhead or 8.7 miles west of the Timber turnoff on the north side of U.S. 26. The trailhead lies on the north side of the Sunset Wayside Nature Study Area, just to the left of the "41st Infantry Division" sign.

Both of these trails are easy to follow, with blue dot markers defining the route.

4-County Point Trail: This path meanders the Wolf Creek riparian environment before it pulls away into the forest. Salal, huckleberry, moss, Oregon grape, and cascading ferns color the forest floor. The large stumps tell of the area's former glory.

At .75 mile, the trail arrives at the 4-County Point Monument and the close of the trail. October 1982 marked the dedication of the plaque. Return by the same route.

Sunset Wayside Nature Trail: This loop trail begins at the bridge crossing South Fork Rock Creek. From here, the trail tours the alder-abundant riparian environment.

Snatches of skid road accompany the discovery of the second-growth forest. The series of interpretive posts introduces old-time logging practices, the use of a log sled, antler rubbings, and other features of the forest.

The companion brochure to the Sunset Wayside Nature Study Area can be obtained from the Oregon State Department of Forestry. It is not available at the trailhead.

Saddle Mountain

3 SADDLE MOUNTAIN

Distance: 5.9 miles round trip (with spur)
Elevation Change: 1600 feet
Difficulty: Strenuous
Map: USGS Saddle Mountain
Water: Available at trailhead
Season: Spring through fall
For More Information: District State Parks Headquarters, Ft. Stevens State Park

Saddle Mountain (elevation 3283 feet) affords some of the best vistas in Oregon's North Coast Range. From the summit, views of four Cascade volcanoes—Mt. Rainier, Mt. Saint Helens, Mt. Adams, and Mt. Hood—enchant the visitor with their snow-covered elegance. To the west are views of the ocean, Astoria, and the mouth of the Columbia River. With a temperature inversion, the summit spectacle features waves of fog drifting inland to claim the river valleys.

While the vista is the primary draw for most hikers, Saddle Mountain is also a significant botanical area, boasting some 300 flora species, including the rare crucifer, believed to grow only in this limited province. Springtime presents a wildflower showcase on the mountain, with Oregon purple iris, cinquefoil, nodding onion, goatsbeard, yellow fawn lily, and false Solomon's seal.

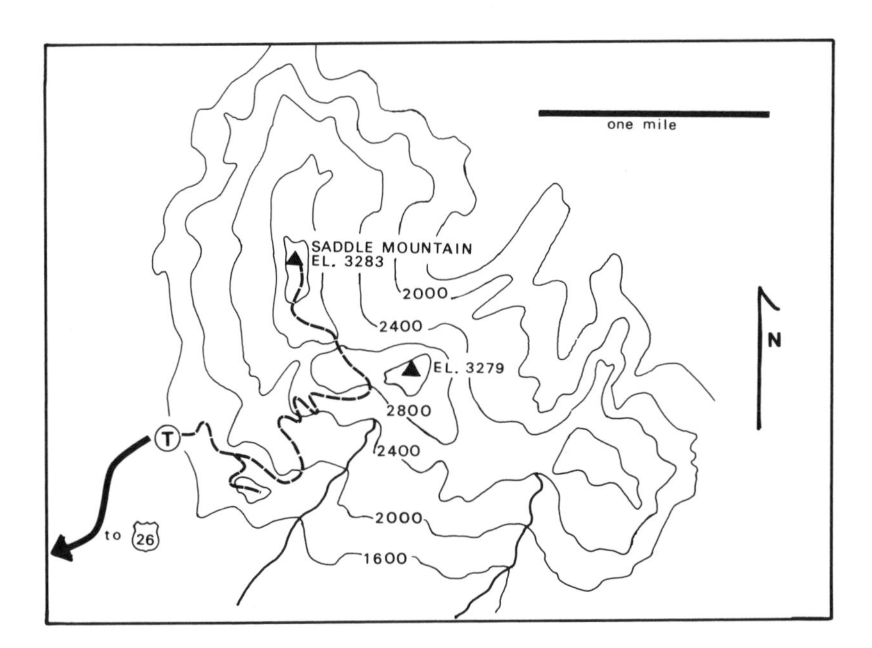

Dubbed "Swallalahoost" by the Indians, Saddle Mountain figures in one of their legends. It is said that from here a great chief ascended in the form of an eagle to become the creator of thunder and lightning. Lewis and Clark mentioned this landmark in their journals, and the Tillamook fire of 1933 was first reported from the summit lookout. This lookout, like many across the country, is now dismantled.

To reach Saddle Mountain from the west, from the junction of U.S. 101 and 26, travel 20 miles east on U.S. 26. From the opposite direction, travel west on U.S. 26 for 17.8 miles beyond the Jewell turnoff. Turn north at the sign for Saddle Mountain State Park. The park lies at the end of the road in 6.9 miles.

On summer weekends, the trail's popularity creates parking chaos. Spillover parking lines the road leading to the park.

From the east side of the parking area, the path begins as a wide paved swath, eventually becoming a trail. In .2 mile a side trail departs to the right. It's a nice .25-mile side-jaunt affording the first vistas of the journey with good views of Saddle Mountain, its pronounced dikes (raised rock veins), and the surrounding Coast Range.

The guide rail to and along this outpost is in disrepair, so use of it to steady your stride merits caution. (Note: The State Parks Division plans extensive rehabilitation of the Saddle Mountain Trail, beginning July 1, 1989.)

Once again on the main trail, the first stretch is mostly shaded.

Second-growth fir and alder stands reign above a varied undergrowth of cow parsnip, maidenhair fern, vine maple, and thimbleberry. A steady stream of hikers courses over the trail. Groups of all ages challenge the summit.

At 1.1 miles, the trail pulls into the open. Shade now is prized. The trail is often gravelly and riddled by shortcuts. To avoid contributing to the growing problem of erosion, hikers should keep to the main trail.

At 2 miles, the trail tops the ridge, with views to the north. Prairie smoke, Siskiyou fritillary, Indian paintbrush, and monkey flowers ornament the slope.

The final .7-mile charge on the summit is slowed by loose, crumbly rock. But the view rewards the effort. The grandeur of the volcano and ocean vistas is compromised only by the broad sweeps of clearcut and the mostly denuded Humbug Mountain. The park land spreading from the summit is primarily second-growth forest, regenerated following the logging of the 1920s and the fires of 1936 and 1939.

Glass fragments provide a clue to the location of the one-time lookout site.

Return by the same route.

4 GALES CREEK TO UNIVERSITY FALLS LOOP

Distance: 12.8 miles round trip
Elevation Change: 1100 feet
Difficulty: Strenuous
Maps: USGS Timber; Tillamook Forest Trails brochure
Water: Available at Gales Creek Park (drinking from streams is not recommended due to Giardia)
Season: All year (in winter, call about possible snow closures)
For More Information: Oregon State Department of Forestry, Forest Grove

In the years 1933, 1939, 1945, and 1951, fire swept what is now Tillamook State Forest. The fire of 1933 alone destroyed nearly 240,000 acres of prime forest.

Today, a thriving second-growth forest greets the visitor. Thanks to a massive rehabilitation effort launched by the state, the land is healing. And, although the recovery is not complete, the forest once again is enjoyable to explore.

University Falls, Tillamook State Forest

Douglas fir, western red cedar, red alder, Oregon grape, sword fern, and salal dominate the vegetation. In the tree plantations, some pines can be seen. Deer, elk, and grouse occasionally reward the quiet hiker.

But University Falls is the highlight of this hike. The viewpoint on the north bank invites quiet appreciation of this rush of water and beauty. The winding course of Elliott Creek adds to the setting's appeal.

In 1987, the volunteer trail coordinators upgraded this trail by eliminating its joint-use segment, which was open to both hikers and off-road vehicles. Now only the road portions of this hike allow ORV use.

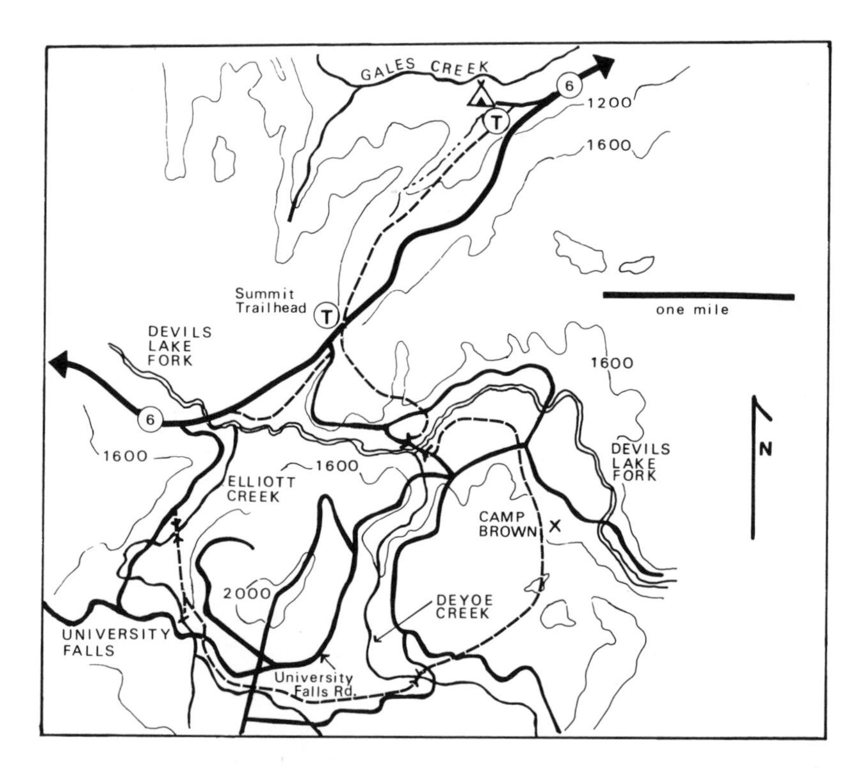

University Falls Loop is reached from Portland by taking U.S. 26 or Oregon 8 west to Oregon 6, the Wilson River Highway. The route continues west on Oregon 6, going 3.6 miles beyond the Timber junction and exiting right for Gales Creek Forest Park. The park is located 1 mile north of Oregon 6. The trailhead is on the left-hand side of the road, 40 yards south of the campground. Hikers may park in the campground.

From the Gales Creek trailhead, the trail switchbacks up a slope, entering a second-growth forest. Soon it traces an old abandoned railroad grade. The moss-overtaken planks separated by animal excavations introduce a rolling footing.

From the railroad grade, the trail parallels a tributary of Gales Creek. Douglas fir, red alder, and some bigleaf maple form the canopy. Salal and Oregon grape alternately ornament the canyon floor. The remaining tall stumps in the area, green with lichen and moss, record the history of the forest: the centuries of undisturbed growth, followed by old-time logging with springboards, followed by fire.

At 1.8 miles, the trail abandons its undulating creekside course and charges uphill to the Summit Trailhead on Oregon 6, climbing 200 feet in .2 mile. To tour the University Falls Loop alone, the hiker can start from the Summit Trailhead for an 8.8-mile loop.

From here, the trail crosses the highway and briefly proceeds up a gravel road. Passing through three gates, the hiker arrives at a gravel lot and a road leading uphill. The trail proper begins to the right, about 75 yards up the road. Blue dot markers and a sign, "Historical Trail," mark the entrance. (The historical-trail designation restricts travel to foot traffic on scenic and historic trails. For the most part, ORV users respect the designation.)

In its 12.8-mile course, the trail crisscrosses several roads. The trail itself is soft-packed forest earth.

At 3.2 miles, the trail arrives at the Devils Lake Fork of the Wilson River, where it now heads downstream to meet the road, crosses the bridge, and returns via the opposite shore.

Later in the hiking season, low waters permit a dry crossing and bypass of this road section. At times of high water, it may be necessary to backtrack up the hill to reach the road and the bridge.

At 4.5 miles, a new section of historical trail avoids the motorcyclists' Camp Brown, cutting up over the knob. While the sounds of ORVs still intrude, the trail is safer and the vegetation undisturbed.

At 5 miles, a hand-dug trail stripes the bed of a reclaimed logging road, where salal and young Douglas fir have overtaken the edges. The easy, even grade and usually peaceful backdrop can lull the hiker into a restful state. Only the raucous call of a Steller's jay breaks one's thoughts.

At 5.8 miles, the trail meets another road. Taking a right, the trail resumes on the left-hand side of the road in 50 yards. Through the alders, the hiker will discover the darkened supports of an old trestle. Elk frequent this area, browsing on the tender young bushes that grow in the creekside environment.

At Deyoe Creek (or Deo Creek per the topo), the water reveals a silty legacy from the fire years and the subsequent cleanups. Near Elliott Creek, the trail skirts another fire-darkened trestle.

At 7.5 miles, the trail meets a road. Turn right and follow the road for a short distance to University Falls Road. Across University Falls Road, the trail resumes, tracing the old wagon road that once led to a camp above the falls. Where the trail comes to a T, approaching the canyon bottom, a left leads to the falls viewpoint. A right leads to the loop's continuance.

Fed by winter rains, this 65-foot falls is a surprising mix of power and grace. In winter, chilling bursts of spray discourage lengthy viewing. Later in the year, more peaceful viewing of a reduced falls is possible. The Elliott Creek Canyon creates a pleasant wooded showcase for this featured attraction.

Going to the right from the T junction, the trail travels a winding course, marked by steep stretches, as it passes from forest to meadow.

After the Elliott Creek footbridge (8.7 miles), the trail graduates into road, for the next mile. Pass the convergence of Elliott Creek and the Devils Lake Fork of the Wilson River and bear left on the main road, climbing above the watercourse to Highway 6. The trail resumes on the east side of the highway's Devils Lake Fork Bridge.

An alternative to this road travel, when water levels permit, is to ford the stream below the convergence, thereby saving .5 mile of walking.

On the opposite shore, the trail once again follows a common-use road until it meets up with Highway 6, in .6 mile. Take a right to reach the Summit Trailhead, located on the north side of the road. Continue downhill along Gales Creek Trail for the conclusion of the hike.

With the trail from the Elliott Creek footbridge to the Summit Trailhead offering little other than exercise and overviews of the watercourses, the Gales Creek Trail concludes the hike with a scenic memory.

5 ELK MOUNTAIN

Distance: 4 miles round trip, or 8.5 miles taking the loop
Elevation Change: 1900 feet (loop: 2000 feet)
Difficulty: Strenuous
Maps: USGS Timber and Enright; Tillamook Forest Trails brochure
Water: Available at campground
Season: Spring through fall
For More Information: Oregon State Department of Forestry, Forest Grove

The highlight of this hike is the panoramic view from and near the summit. On a clear day, you can see three volcanoes (Mts. Adams, Hood, and Jefferson), the Cascades, the Willamette Valley, and the ridges of the Coast Range. The openness of this area, a product of the fire years 1933, 1939, and 1945, delivers additional vantage points along the trail.

The fires that plagued this region rank among the great disasters to have struck the Northwest. Together, the fires destroyed some 356,000 acres of prime forest habitat.

The snags of the upper elevations recall the fire years. The forest "sameness" recalls the reforestation effort. Beneath the Douglas fir–hemlock forest, the vegetation is primarily Oregon

Elk Mountain

grape and salal, with a sprinkling of fern and blackberry.

To reach this trail from Portland, travel west on U.S. 26 or Oregon 8 to Oregon 6, the Wilson River Highway. Continue west on Oregon 6 for 10.8 miles beyond the Timber Junction. Turn right (north) at the sign for Elk Creek Forest Park. The campground is in .3 mile. The trailhead lies at the far end of the campground, just across the bridge, on the left-hand side of the road.

Blue dot markers identify the trail route, which quickly reveals its steep, upward character. Red alder and ferns and the sound of Elk Creek provide the backdrop for the first leg of the hike. At .25 mile, the hiker comes to a small saddle. From here, the trail cuts upward to the right. There is a trail sign at this junction, but it is loosely wired and may not last long.

Just above the saddle, the hiker arrives at the first viewpoint, with an overlook of Wilson River Canyon. The river already lies well below the hiker. The mountains to the west and the snags on the rocky slopes add to the vista. The sounds from the highway grow faint. In another quarter mile, a second vantage is secured.

As the trail winds to the north slope, the vegetation becomes thicker. But shade sources remain few. Carry plenty of water.

Topping the ridge, the trail flattens out and snakes its way toward a false top (1.5 miles). A brief detour from the trail delivers prized vistas from this rocky outpost.

The main trail continues, encircling the base of the false summit, delivering views of Elk and Kings mountains. The summit of Elk Mountain lies ahead in .5 mile. Snags punctuate the skyline. The fire-denuded tops of these mountains reveal the rugged character of the Coast Range, a feature often masked by the forested slopes.

The wind-whipped summit offers expansive viewing of the Cascades, spotlighting Mt. Adams and Mt. Hood, with the serial ridges of the Coast Range and the broad Willamette Valley competing for equal time. The summit's grassy top welcomes repose.

Scattered elk track and flattened grasses lend support to the mountain's name. Thistle, paintbrush, and daisy touch color to the summit.

For the return trip, the hiker can either retrace the trail just walked, or strike out on the loop trail, which utilizes logging roads to complete the majority of its distance.

Elk Creek, Elk Mountain Trail

For the loop, the path is indicated by the downward-canted trail sign. As the sign hints, the next .6 mile offers steep and rugged going. Although marked, the trail has the feel of a cross-country jaunt. Exercise caution and keep a sharp eye out for markers. It's easy to miss a switchback here.

At 2.6 miles (measured from trailhead), the trail merges with an old logging road that switchbacks up the next ridge, rising well above Elk Mountain. Where the road pulls into the open, views of Mt. Hood and Mt. Jefferson greet the hiker. The trail then descends to a saddle and a road junction at 4.2 miles. The road to the left leads to neighboring Kings Mountain, Hike 6. The road to the right leads to the loop's continuance.

Cutting down from the junction saves 1.5 miles of road travel. It's steep but not compared to much of the hike. Well-padded game trails lead the way.

Opting against this shortcut, at 5 miles you arrive at the road junction for Elk Creek Campground and take a right.

Hiking the logging road to the campground, one obtains some nice overviews of Elk Creek. In a few places, the debris from the succession of fires and cleanups has spoiled the creek canyon. Elsewhere, alders overhang and shadow the creek, while sword ferns spray over the rocks. Agate, jasper, and quartz attract the rockhound.

At 8.5 miles, the loop concludes at the trailhead.

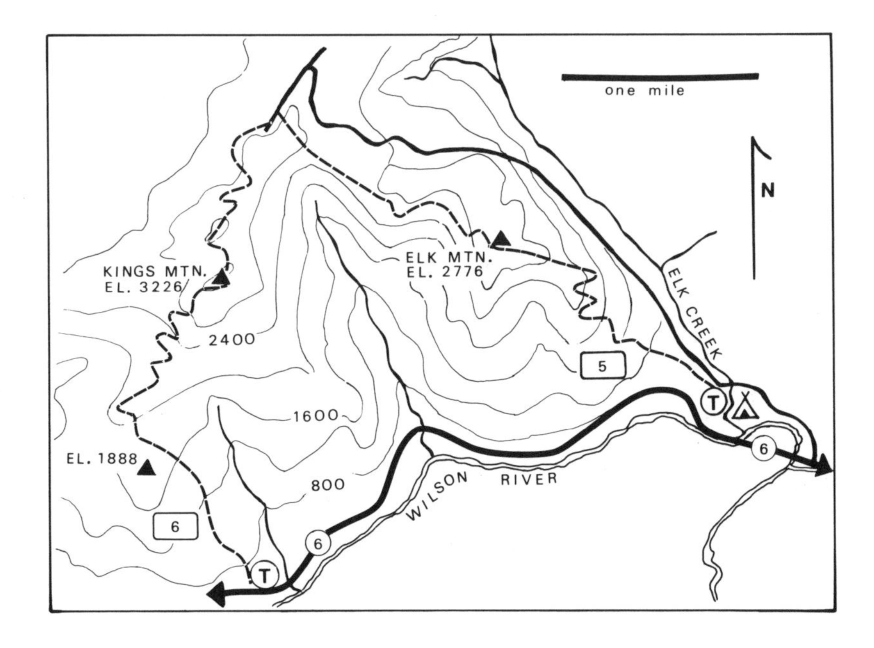

6 KINGS MOUNTAIN

Distance: 5 miles round trip (with options to extend hike)
Elevation Change: 2600 feet
Difficulty: Strenuous
Maps: USGS Enright; Tillamook Forest Trails brochure
Water: Carry water
Season: Spring through fall
For More Information: Oregon State Department of Forestry, Forest Grove

See map on page 37.

In the early 1900s, a reporter wrote this about the area: "From the summit of the Coast Range to the tidewater lines, it is simply one vast and dense forest." Back then, who would have guessed what history held in store for this prized forest land? In 1933, 1939, 1945, and 1951, fire swept over the four-county area in what was to become known as the "six-year jinx." The devastation is known today as the "Tillamook Burn."

In the years following the fires, the state undertook a massive rehabilitation program, building roads, cutting snags, planting trees, and building trails. Everyone from schoolchildren to convicts played a role in the restoration process. Finally, in 1973 the stigma of the jinx and the burn was lifted with the area officially renamed Tillamook State Forest.

On the trail to Kings Mountain, the progress of the rehabilitation effort can be witnessed in the young forest. In what proved a pioneering use of the helicopter in forest management, the smaller trees near the ridge represent helicopter seedings.

The summit boasts grand views of the Coast Range, the Wilson River Valley, and the Cascades.

To reach the Kings Mountain Trailhead, from Portland, take U.S. 26 or Oregon 8 west to Oregon 6, the Wilson River Highway. Continue west on Oregon 6, going 13.5 miles beyond the Timber junction. The signed trailhead lies on the north side of the road.

From Oregon 6, the trail immediately ducks into a red alder–maple woodland. Sword fern, moss-topped logs, and time-touched stumps please the eye. The muffled song of a small creek west of the trail occasionally rides the breeze.

As the trail zigzags up the south flank of Kings Mountain, it makes frequent use of skid roads, remnants from the logging days. At .3 mile the trail breaks into character, with a spurt of no-nonsense ascent. Second-growth firs gradually replace the deciduous woodland.

Early on, the trail's steep charges are balanced by relatively even grades, where the leg muscles and respiration rate can calm down. In the final attack on the summit, such reprieves do not exist.

Snags atop Kings Mountain

At 1.2 miles, the trail pulls out of the tree cover and into the open. Bracken fern, thistle, foxglove, and daisies adorn the slope. From here, enjoy overviews of Tillamook State Forest, the Wilson River Valley, and the ridges of the Coast Range, with hints of better views to come. Early-morning hikers sometimes startle deer and grouse along the trail.

At 2 miles, the trail grows steeper. From mid- to late summer, thimbleberry, huckleberry, and trailing blackberry offer a satisfying nibble to the weary traveler. Silver snags pierce the summer sky.

At 2.4 miles, the hiker reaches the primary summit of Kings Mountain. A second summit lies .1 mile beyond. In the open meadow Columbia lily, gentian, daisy, thistle, yarrow, and Indian paintbrush parade their colors. Huckleberry bushes abound. Tracks and matted grasses betray the recent presence of elk upon the lofty post. Hummingbirds buzz the top.

Views of Elk Mountain, Mt. Saint Helens, Mt. Adams, Mt. Hood, and the neighboring features of the Coast Range welcome a lengthy summit stay.

Return by the same route. The hardy may continue, however, by following the trail downhill off the second summit to the Elk Mountain Trail, Hike 5.

For the first .3 mile, this trial descends sharply and is partially overgrown. It then undulates below a ridge, before charging to the top at 3.3 miles. From the ridge, it's a .4-mile descent to the saddle and the road junction for Elk and Kings mountains.

From here, there are several options, depending on whether you wish to visit Elk Mountain and whether a car shuttle to the Elk Creek Campground has been previously arranged. But, however long the hike, carry plenty of water; the sun and physical exertion demand it.

7 NEAHKAHNIE MOUNTAIN

Distance: 3 miles round trip, or 5.5 miles taking a loop via the South Sand Beach Trail and U.S. 101
Elevation Change: 1100 feet
Difficulty: Moderate
Maps: USGS Nehalem, Cannon Beach
Water: Carry water
Season: All year
For More Information: District State Parks Headquarters, Nehalem Bay State Park

Steeped in legend, Neahkahnie Mountain has long intrigued and seduced the historian and the treasure hunter. According to Indian oral history, in the early 1700s a Spanish galleon (believed to be the *San Francisco Xavier*) shipwrecked near the base

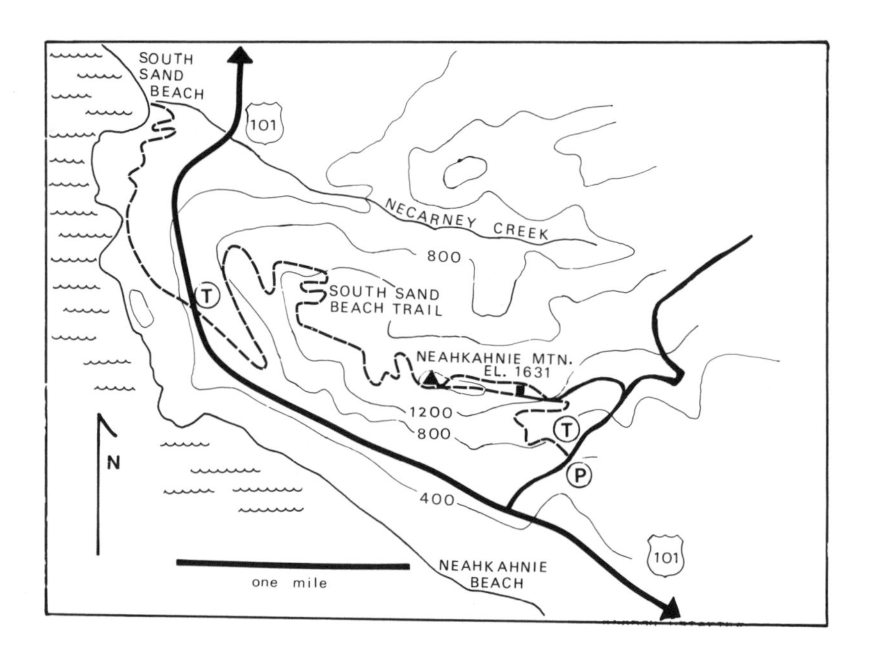

Neahkahnie Mountain Trail

of Neahkahnie Mountain. Here, the marooned sailors reportedly buried the galleon treasure. Beachcomber discoveries of beeswax candles, known to be among the ship's cargo, have fanned the hopes of treasure hunters.

But the undisputed treasure of Neahkahnie Mountain is the vista secured from its summit (elevation 1631 feet). From this lofty post, one can view the Nehalem River flood plain, Nehalem Bay, the beach and coastal communities to the south, and the ceaseless ridges of the Coast Range.

Wild rose, foxglove, goatsbeard, wild onions, and thimbleberry ornament Neahkahnie's cap. And in the spring, the pink coast fawn lily adds its beauty.

The Neahkahnie Mountain trailhead is conveniently located off U.S. 101, 1.2 miles north of the Neahkahnie Beach exit (just north of Manzanita), or 2.2 miles south of Oswald West State Park Campground.

On the east side of U.S. 101, an 8-foot cedar post indicates the trail and the entrance to a gravel road, as does a green-and-white hiker sign. The gravel road continues east for .4 mile to trailhead parking on the right. The trail begins on the left.

Following part of an old Indian trail, the trail switches up a brushy slope dotted with red alder and spruce. Almost immediately views open up of the shoreline, the bay, and the beach community, with promises of more to come. The muffled roar of the ocean and birds rustling in the brush accompany the steps of the hiker.

The brushy slope, normally an adversary to the hiker, is in this case an ally, creating open expanses for uninterrupted viewing.

At .5 mile, the trail takes a couple of quick switchbacks. Here the trees are larger and the groundcover more varied, with mosses, ferns, and Oregon grape. As the trail continues toward the ridge, stands of Sitka spruce block the view.

At 1 mile, the trail arrives atop the ridge at a junction. To reach the summit, head west along the road or follow the South Sand Beach Trail. Either way is .5 mile.

The road west ends in .1 mile, near the TV switching station. The trail may be picked up around the building to the left. The trail traces the spine of the ridge, offering views from each of three knobs along the spine. The second and third knobs sport geodetic markers. Tangles of salal encroach the narrow path.

Alternatively, the South Sand Beach Trail tours Neahkahnie's north flank just below the ridge. Windows in the second-growth Sitka spruce provide glimpses of the coast stretching to the north. At .5 mile the trail cuts up over the ridge just east of the third knob (the summit).

On a clear winter day, this post promises a good vantage for whalewatching. The rhythm and voice of the ocean drive away thought and soothe the spirit, encouraging a leisurely stay.

From the summit, either return by the same route or via the South Sand Beach Trail and U.S. 101 to make a loop.

Forming the loop, the South Sand Beach Trail descends the mountain with long switchbacks. The forest on the west flank is more varied, with hemlock and Douglas fir sharing the slope with the Sitka spruce. Salal, Oregon grape, moss, and sword fern blanket the forest floor.

About .5 mile from the summit, openings in the trees provide views of the mouth of the Nehalem River and the headlands punctuating the coast.

The trail continues winding north through the forest, before emptying onto an open grassy slope. Here, views of Cape Falcon hold the hiker. The trail remains in the open, reaching U.S. 101 at 3.8 miles.

From the South Sand Beach–101 trailhead, a distance of 1.3 miles south along U.S. 101 and .4 mile east along the gravel road awaits. But splendid coastal scenery is the hiker's companion.

Hebo Lake, Pioneer-Indian Trail

8 PIONEER-INDIAN TRAIL

Distance: 16 miles round trip or an 8-mile shuttle
Elevation Change: 1500 feet
Difficulty: Strenuous
Maps: USGS Grand Ronde and Hebo; USFS Siuslaw National Forest
Water: Hebo Lake Campground, summer only
Season: All year (in winter, call about possible closure due to intermittent snow)
For More Information: Hebo Ranger District

This 8-mile trail traces a segment of the old Grand Ronde Indian trail linking the Willamette and Tillamook valleys. In 1854, pioneer Hiram Smith developed the transportation route, and the trail remained in use until 1882, when the Little Nestucca River Wagon Road opened.

In 1975, Forest Service employee Leonard Whitmore stumbled upon the historic trail and set about restoring its identifiable segments. The year 1984 brought about the construction of additional trail to link these historic pieces.

The Hebo area, which was ravaged by fire in 1845 and again in 1910, today offers a healthy second-growth Douglas fir forest, bracken fern meadows, and broad summit meadows brimming with wild strawberry and housing the rare silver spot butterfly.

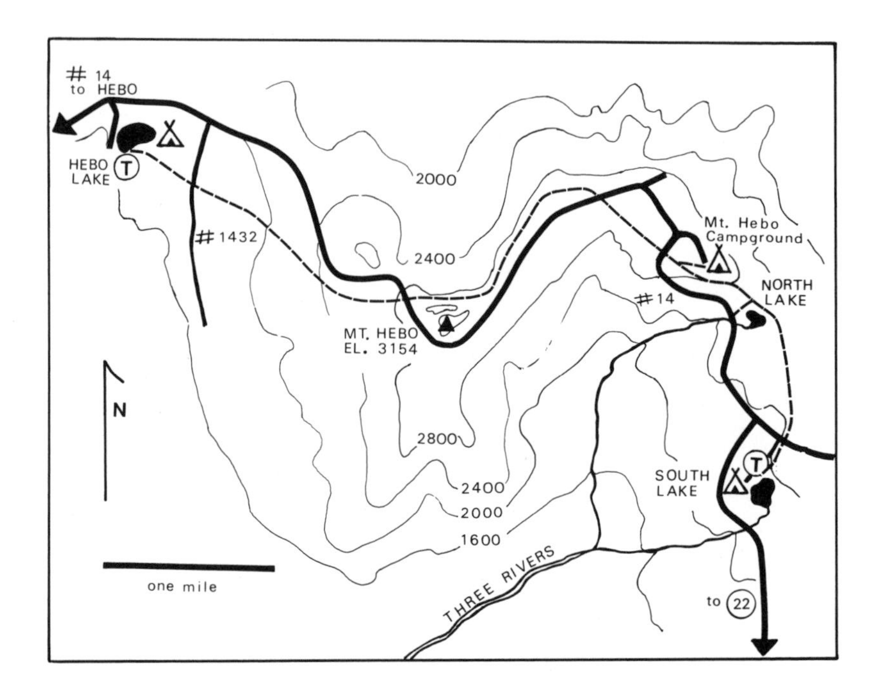

The trail connects three mountain lakes (Hebo, North, and South lakes)—a rarity for the Coast Range. And its twisting course delivers exceptional ocean, valley, and Coast Range vistas.

To explore this historic route, take Forest SR 14 east from Oregon 22 at Hebo. The turn is just north of the ranger station. Continue for 4.5 miles and turn south to Hebo Lake Campground. The trailhead lies on the southside of the campground. It's marked, and there's a nearby parking area.

For shuttle hiking, the last trailhead is located at South Lake. From Hebo Lake Campground, continue uphill on Forest SR 14 for 7.3 miles taking a right onto Forest SR 1428. In .3 mile, turn right to South Lake Campground, and the trailhead. The road to South Lake is graveled, narrow, and sometimes rough.

Beginning from the Hebo Lake trailhead, the hiker gains an acquaintance with the region through a series of interpretive signboards telling of the vegetation, the burn, and the reforestation. Sitka spruce, young Douglas fir, and an occasional ash line the trail. The groundcover explodes in a profusion of green, with *Maianthemum,* oxalis, twisted stalk, false Solomon's seal, and bracken fern.

At 1 mile the trail crosses a fading, grass-overtaken road, which welcomes additional exploration. The trail then alternates between woodlands and small meadows, before entering a larger homestead meadow. Here, a herd of 20 to 25 elk can sometimes be spotted in the early morning. Posts at both ends of the meadow mark the line of the trail.

From the homestead meadow the trail begins to climb, reaching Forest SR 14 at 2.8 miles. Vanilla leaf dominates just prior to the road. The next .75 mile is on the old lookout road. An overgrown spur charges up the slope to the summit of Mt. Hebo, but the main trail furnishes equally rewarding views. Thimbleberry, salmonberry, and lupine crowd the road.

At 3.6 miles, a narrow corridor of berry bushes funnels the hiker to an open mountain meadow and views of the Tillamook and Nestucca valleys. Wild strawberry abounds in the meadow. The trail again crosses Forest SR 14 at 4.5 miles. From there the trail angles uphill and to the left.

The trail briefly returns to a forest of cedar, Sitka spruce, and salal, then empties onto an open plateau. The plateau, littered with silvered snags and downfalls, offers prized views on clear days. The location is ideal for a midday repast.

Leaving the plateau, the trail crosses the road to North and South lakes. At 5.2 miles the trail splits. To the left lies Mt. Hebo Campground in .2 mile. The main trail continues right, tracing the south slope of an open ridge. The hiker exchanges views of the Mt. Hebo summit for views to the south and east, including the drainages of the Salmon and Yamhill rivers. Indian paintbrush

Elk

and penstemon, anchored in the rock crevices, bring color to the trail.

The trail then switchbacks downhill to the lakes. It's a steep descent through Douglas fir forest with an understory of sword and bracken fern and red huckleberry.

At 6.6 miles, the trail splits, with the left fork continuing on to South Lake and the right fork leading to North Lake (.1 mile). Vegetation has begun to reclaim the North Lake perimeter, and a thick tangle of bushes defies easy access except along the road.

Nearing South Lake, the many snags common to the North Lake area disappear. A resurgence in the variety of the plant complex occurs, with *Maianthemum,* false Solomon's seal, and vanilla leaf threading through the salal and Oregon grape.

After crossing Forest SR 14, the trail delivers the hiker to the South Lake trailhead, following a short, steep descent.

9 HEBO PLANTATION

Distance: 2 miles round trip
Elevation Change: 500 feet
Difficulty: Easy
Map: USFS Siuslaw National Forest
Water: Carry water
Season: All year
For More Information: Hebo Ranger District

In 1845 and 1910, fire swept the slopes of Mt. Hebo. After the fire of 1910, the United States Forest Service launched an ambitious 20-year reforestation effort that planted some 8000 acres with Douglas fir and a mix of pine, spruce, and hardwood. This trail tours some of those planted acres.

Beautiful carved wooden signboards introduce the features of this trail and identify the planting schemes. Despite an often detected regimen of rows, the plantation trail retains a wild character with its rush of groundcover—a rush that sometimes surpasses the schedule of regular maintenance.

Of the Douglas fir plantings, those grown in Idaho and Washington did not fare as well as those native to the Oregon Coast Range.

To learn the lessons of this nature trail and to draw from its tranquility, turn east onto Forest SR 14 from Oregon 22 at Hebo. The turn is just north of the ranger station. The first trailhead lies 3.1 miles ahead on Forest SR 14. The second trailhead is at 3.6 miles. Both are marked.

Reforestation success of Hebo Plantation Nature Trail

Beginning from the easternmost trailhead, the hiker is immediately greeted with a wealth of undergrowth: sword and bracken fern, salmonberry, false Solomon's seal, *Maianthemum,* vanilla leaf, and twisted stalk. Beneath the thriving army of trees, the forest floor is a host of shapes, textures, and shades. A small intermittent creek feeds this bounty, sometimes muddying the trail. Nettles add to the undergrowth tangle.

Elk tracks riddle the trail, and the thick bushes promise concealed rabbits. The trail assumes a downhill character, which becomes more pronounced where the trail parallels and paces off the length of a downfall at .4 mile.

The trail then levels out, as it enters the Douglas fir yield study. This sample plot was established in 1934. At .9 mile, the trail delivers the hiker to the moss-etched interpretive sign marked "Crop Tree Pruning." From here the trail ascends back to Forest SR 14. Return the way you came or via the road.

10 BASKETT BUTTE/ MORGAN LAKE

Distance: 5 miles round trip
Elevation Change: 200 feet
Difficulty: Moderate
Map: Willamette Valley National Wildlife Refuges brochure
Water: Carry water
Season: May through September (with Baskett Butte Loop open year-round)
For More Information: Refuge Manager, William L. Finley National Wildlife Refuge

Named for an early horse rancher, this 2492-acre refuge is part of the greater Willamette Valley National Wildlife Refuge complex, supplying winter habitat for dusky Canada geese. The valley's urban sprawl and intensive agricultural practices robbed the goose of much of its traditional winter ground, prompting the establishment of these protected lands in the mid-1960s. Oregon's Willamette Valley is host to nearly all of the wintering dusky population.

Because of its more northerly location and because of its large body of water, Morgan Lake, the duskies and other waterfowl linger weeks longer at this refuge than at either the Ankeny or William L. Finley refuges. Baskett Slough's rolling hills, grasslands, and ancient lakebed create a diverse habitat, supporting some 200 species of wildlife.

During the wintering season, access to the refuge (save for Baskett Butte Loop) is limited to reduce man's impact on the duskies. But wintering season and hunting season for other game and waterfowl overlap.

From the junction of Oregon 99W and Oregon 22, west of Salem, take Oregon 99W north 1.7 miles, turning west onto Coville Road. There's a sign here for Baskett Slough National Wildlife Refuge. Go 1.4 miles down Coville Road; trailhead parking is on the right. Public-use hours are from sunrise to sunset.

The mowed track of the trail leads into the refuge. In a short distance, the hiker arrives at a junction. Taking the left toward the viewpoint (and Baskett Butte) introduces the walker to some Willamette Valley splendor—grassland, wild roses, blackberries, and young oaks. The clicking of crickets and perhaps the whirr of a distant tractor engine contribute to the valley's song.

During the summer, the trail is sunny and humid with few patches of shade. Best hours for hiking are found at the edges of day.

At a quarter mile, a spur departs the trail to the left, leading to an overlook of the valley in 200 yards. The primary trail bears right.

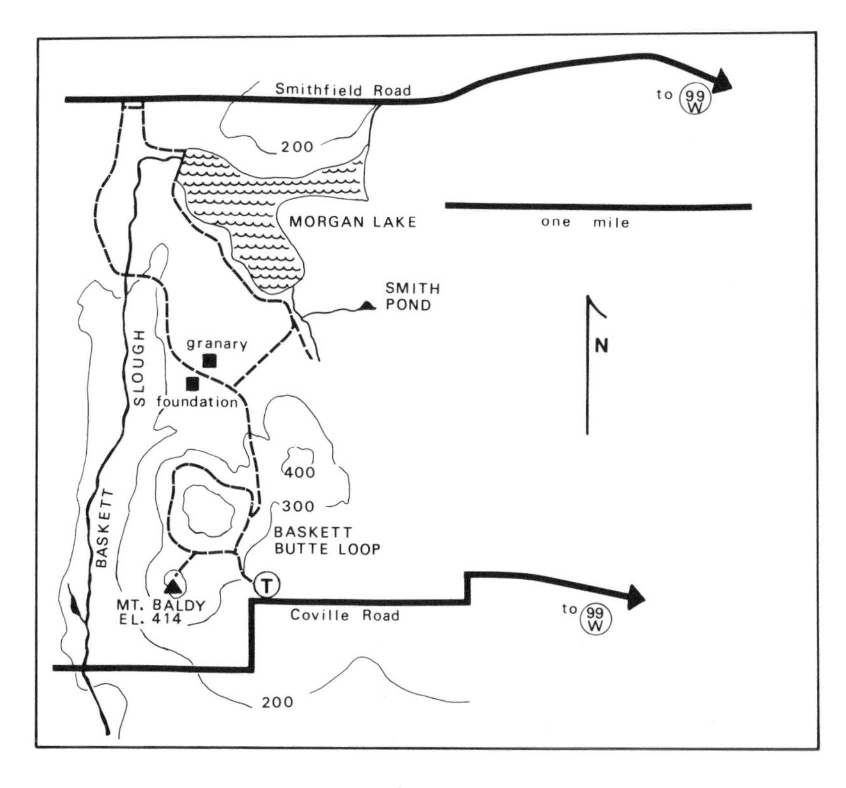

Speckling the path to the viewpoint are dwarf star tulips and buttercups. Patchwork fields, farm buildings, the foothills of the Coast Range, and Marys Peak, to the south, contribute to the vista. Poison oak shoots push up through the grasses along the trail's edge.

Returning to the primary trail to Baskett Butte, in a short distance, the hiker enters the cloaking tangle of oaks, maples, and other deciduous trees. At .8 mile, the trail leaves the woodland, arriving at another trail junction. Going right returns the hiker to the parking area (.4 mile). Going left continues the exploration with a tour of Morgan Lake and Baskett Slough.

Hawks, swallows, alligator lizards, and black-tail deer often add to the hiker's reward. At 1.25 miles, just prior to reaching the refuge outbuilding, a right turn leads to the 3-mile Morgan Lake Loop.

Following in a counterclockwise direction, at 1.7 miles the hiker spies the lake, and in another 100 yards the trail comes to a T. The branch to the right traces a field boundary south. Continuing left alongside the hedgerow, leads to Morgan Lake, where the trail rounds the lake's west shore and offers close-up viewing.

Morgan Lake, Baskett Slough National Wildlife Refuge

The trail then cuts away from the lake, slicing the edge of a field. At 2.9 miles, the trail meets the spur from the Smithfield Road trailhead. The main trail continues left to the refuge gravel road paralleling Baskett Slough. A second left at the road leads to the close of the loop and the return to the Baskett Butte trailhead.

At 3.1 miles, cattails abound, bending in the wind. Everywhere in the refuge, hawks patrol, swoop, and dive, sometimes receiving the angry escort of small birds. At 4.25 miles is the granary, a favorite nesting site for cliff swallows. From here, it's a .75-mile trek back to the parking area or a 1.25-mile trip retracing the Baskett Butte segment.

11 VALLEY OF THE GIANTS

Distance: 1.7 miles round trip
Elevation Change: 200 feet
Difficulty: Easy
Map: USFS Siuslaw National Forest
Water: North Fork Siletz River
Season: All year (in winter, call regarding snowfall and road conditions)
For More Information: Bureau of Land Management, Salem

This remote Coast Range grove receives protection because it harbors Oregon's largest known stand of record-sized Douglas firs. Salem's big-tree champion, Maynard Drawson, deserves the credit for spurring the Bureau of Land Management (BLM) to set aside this 47-acre preserve. Highlighting the grove are at least a dozen trees with girths of more than 25 feet and many others that push that mark. Clearcuts and second-growth forests encircle the grove—the decision to preserve it came just in time.

The now tumbled "Big Guy" once presided over the Valley of the Giants Trail. Before falling victim to a winter storm in 1984, this 600-year-old tree ranked among the largest known standing Douglas firs, with a 230-foot height and a 36.5-foot girth.

The original trail, built in 1976 as a BLM-sponsored Youth Conservation Corps effort, has been expanded to incorporate a loop. The Chemeketans, a Salem-based hiking club, help maintain the trail.

The one drawback to this hike is the maze of back roads that must be negotiated to reach the trailhead.

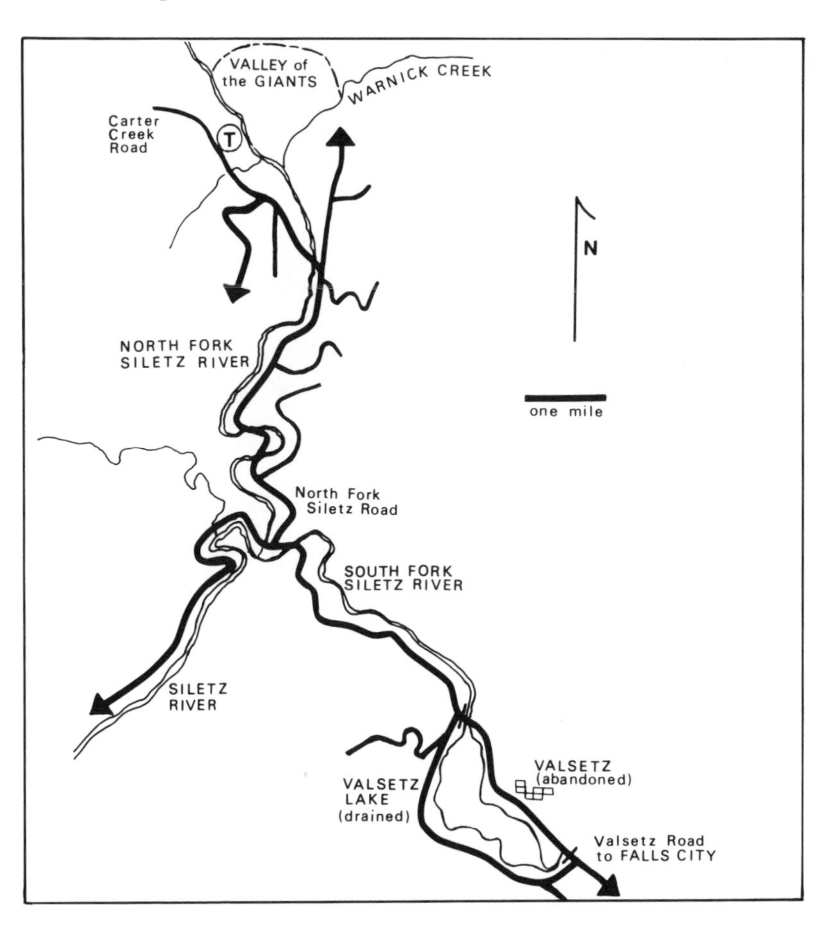

Old-growth Douglas fir, Valley of the Giants

Beginning from the west end of Falls City (located west of Salem), take Bridge Street south. The sign at the junction indicates this road goes to Pedee and Camp Kilowan. In less than 1 mile, the road turns to gravel. In a little more than a mile, the road surface becomes heavy gravel. Here, the name changes to Valsetz Road.

This is a logging road, with truck traffic on weekdays. The wide road, however, easily accommodates two-lane travel. Packed dirt replaces the heavy gravel at about 6 miles. At Valsetz (14.75 miles), gates and signs route travel around the former lake's southwest end. Where the road comes to an abrupt T, hikers take a right.

The road along the lakebed's south border is riddled with potholes, but remains passable for conventional vehicles. At the end of the lake, bear right. In 5 miles, the road crosses the South Fork Siletz bridge.

Going .3 mile beyond the bridge, take a right up the hill on the North Fork Siletz Road. Where the road forks, in about 5 miles, continue left, keeping to the main road. The main road soon crosses the North Fork Siletz bridge. One mile from this bridge, take a right onto Carter Creek Road. The trailhead turnout lies .5 mile downhill, on the right.

As the Siuslaw National Forest map does not include the roads beyond Valsetz Lake, it's important to watch the odometer closely and be alert for the indicated turns.

From the trailhead turnout, the old logging road to the right introduces the trail. Fern, hemlock, and fir crowd the abandoned roadbed. In a quarter mile, the actual trail begins on the right, heading downhill to the North Fork Siletz River.

The wide back of a Douglas fir offers a dry crossing, as the old-growth preserve beckons from the opposite shore. Its skyline of 200-foot-high Douglas firs chokes out much of the sunlight, but oxalis, moss, and dripping lichen thrive beneath the canopy. The rich smell of life and decay fills the air.

At a half mile, a fallen giant interrupts the trail. Here, the hiker must either cross under or over and through the fall and a second downed tree, a fairly easy task. Once on the opposite side of the log, the .7-mile loop begins. One spur leads toward the river, a second up the slope near the roots of the fallen tree.

Taking the left spur toward the river, the hiker witnesses some excellent examples of nurse trees. The trail itself is nicely structured, wherever possible retaining the fallen trees. With the shortness of the trail, the hiker can well afford the added effort needed to pass these trees since they help retain the naturalness of the setting.

At .75 mile (distance measured from the trailhead), the hiker comes to a downed tree that appears to mark the end of the trail. Looking down the log to the right, however, one notices a cutout. The cutout holds steps leading to the trail's continuance.

At .8 mile, the "Big Guy" greets the hiker. The trail at one time stopped here, but now continues to form a loop.

With the trees dominant overhead, it is easy to overlook the small-scale treasures of this hike. Walking the loop twice or approaching it from the opposite end delivers new perspectives. The smallness of this preserve (47 acres) also invites cross-country exploration. For those less skilled in the outdoors, the river is a natural guide.

12 SECTION 36 LOOP

Distance: 4.3 miles round trip, or 5.5 miles round trip with the Arboretum Loop side excursion
Elevation Change: 900 feet
Difficulty: Moderate
Map: The Section 36 Loop Trail Guide
Water: Available at Forestry Club Cabin
Season: All year
For More Information: OSU Research Forest

Peavy Arboretum is part of a 12,000-acre research forest maintained by the College of Forestry at Oregon State University (OSU). Its grounds hold a nearly complete inventory of woody plants from the Pacific Northwest, as well as plants from across the United States and around the world. Native Coast Range vegetation is interspersed among the exotic plantings.

Completed in 1982 and extended in 1987, the Section 36 Loop Trail unites the Calloway Creek and Pine Race Study trails of the 1920s. It also ties together a recent clearcut, an old-growth forest, and Cronemiller Lake.

The Forestry Club Cabin, which launches this trail, was built in 1950 to replace the original 1925 cabin, which was lost due to fire.

Located north of Corvallis, Peavy Arboretum is reached via Oregon 99W. From the south, turn west onto Arboretum Road 1.2

Old foundation along Section 36 Loop, Peavy Arboretum

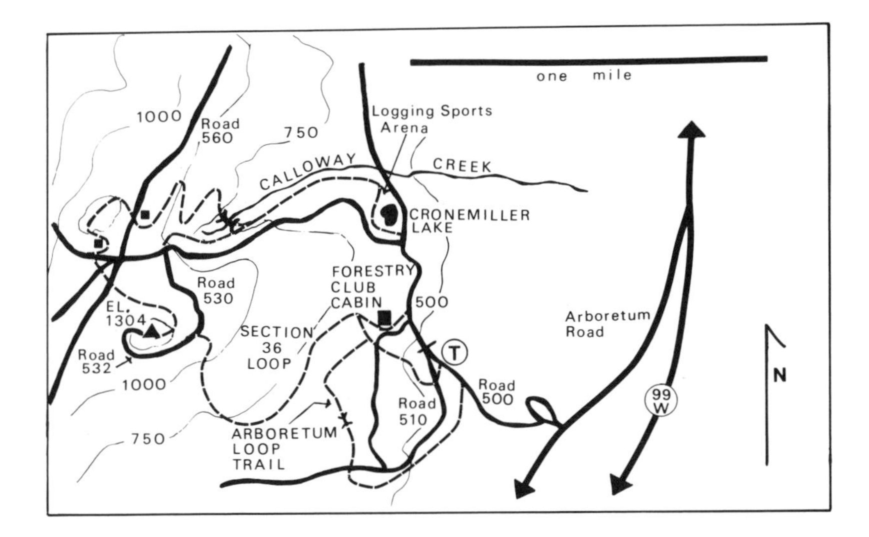

miles north of the intersection of Oregon 99W and Lewisburg Avenue. From the north, turn west onto Arboretum Road .8 mile south of the intersection of Oregon 99W and Tampico Road. Peavy Arboretum lies on the west side of Arboretum Road in .8 mile (equidistant from either Arboretum Road entrance).

Once at the Arboretum, take a left turn at the entry and follow Road 500. In .3 mile, a sign on the left, "Trail to Forestry Cabin," marks the path leading to Section 36 Loop. Arboretum hours are sunrise to sunset.

The Forestry Cabin Trail enters a second-growth forest and soon meets Road 510. Turn right, and walk up the road about 100 feet to resume the trail on the left.

At the upcoming junction with the newly built 1.2-mile Arboretum Loop Trail, continue straight ahead for the cabin and Section 36 Loop. Or, take a left for the 1.2-mile side trip exploring a second-growth forest, a beautiful cedar stand, a riparian environment, and a portion of the research forest, before returning via Road 500.

Forgoing this side trip and continuing straight, at .4 mile, the hiker arrives at the junction for the Forestry Cabin and Section 36 Loop. Before going left for a clockwise tour of the 3.5-mile loop, detour right 100 yards to pick up a Section 36 Loop trail guide at the cabin trailhead. Drinking water and pit toilets are available on the cabin grounds for visitor convenience.

From the Cabin–Section 36 junction, the Section 36 Loop Trail winds its way to the Ponderosa Pine Study Area and to a classic "hooter" tree, an old-growth Douglas fir with multiple branchings. The guideposts along the way introduce the study projects

Moss-draped forest of Section 36 Loop, Peavy Arboretum

and methods, while rustic benches invite a pause and study of the research forest. The trail is well marked.

One-third of the way into the loop, the trail begins to climb, skirting a recent clearcut. Reaching the ridge, the trail briefly joins an old section of Road 530. Summertime hikers will want to carry plenty of water for the upcoming open stretch of trail.

At interpretive post #10, the trail turns left onto Road 532, climbing .3 mile to the clearcut summit and a vista point. Here, the hiker secures sweeping views of the mid-Willamette Valley, stretching from Dallas to Philomath. Only the few remaining snags puncture the vista. This 180-degree Willamette Valley panorama numbers among the finest valley vistas to be found.

From the gravel pad of the summit, the trail angles downhill and to the left. In .3 mile, the trail crosses Nettleton Road, and quickly thereafter Road 580, to re-enter the forest. Where the trail crosses Road 582, turn left and pick up the trail on the opposite side, 10 yards down.

From here, the trail works its way up the hill, bypassing an old foundation. Additional views of the valley and the Coast Range to the west reward the climb. The trail rounds the hilltop, then descends, eventually crossing Road 560.

Re-entering the second-growth forest just to the right of a metal hut, the trail switchbacks downhill to Calloway Creek and Schaefer bridge. Once across the bridge, the trail turns left, touring the old-growth habitat of the north slope. Past trail problems with mud and water have been resolved with new routes and drainages.

The creek setting is captivating, as the moss-draped vine maples create a phantasmagoria of twisted, interlocking beauty. The shaded gallery provides a dramatic contrast to the sun-drenched clearcut slope and the sparse groundcover of the second-growth forest. Sword fern and Oregon grape explode in green profusion, while a woodpecker's tapping and the babble of Calloway Creek add to the trail's sensory appeal.

From the old-growth reserve, the trail continues on to the Logging Sports Arena, where the traditional woodsmen contests continue to be staged by the OSU Forestry Club. Awaiting ahead is Cronemiller Lake, a dammed lake and water source for the research forest. The resident ducks and frogs promise an entertaining performance.

From the lake, turn right onto Road 500 and continue downhill to the cabin. The return to the vehicle is via the Forestry Cabin Trail.

13 MUDDY CREEK TO PIGEON BUTTE

Distance: 4.6 miles round trip
Elevation Change: 300 feet
Difficulty: Easy
Map: Willamette Valley National Wildlife Refuges brochure
Water: Carry water
Season: May through October
For More Information: William L. Finley National Wildlife Refuge

This trail tours part of the Muddy Creek shoreline and passes field and pond before delivering the hiker to the summit of Pigeon Butte (elevation 543 feet). Pigeon Butte is the most prominent feature of the 5325-acre refuge.

Summer-nesting wood ducks and hooded mergansers find suitable sites along the shores of Muddy Creek. Sometimes, this silty waterway plays host to the river otter. But ruffled grouse, California quail, red-tailed hawks, mourning doves, and red-winged blackbirds are more frequently sighted.

The beautiful oak woodland atop the butte offers an inviting retreat. Vistas from Pigeon Butte spotlight the refuge, the Muddy Creek drainage, the Willamette Valley, and the foothills of the Coast Range.

This trail is closed to visitors during the wintering season of the duskies. This closure reduces the disturbance to this subspecies of Canada geese.

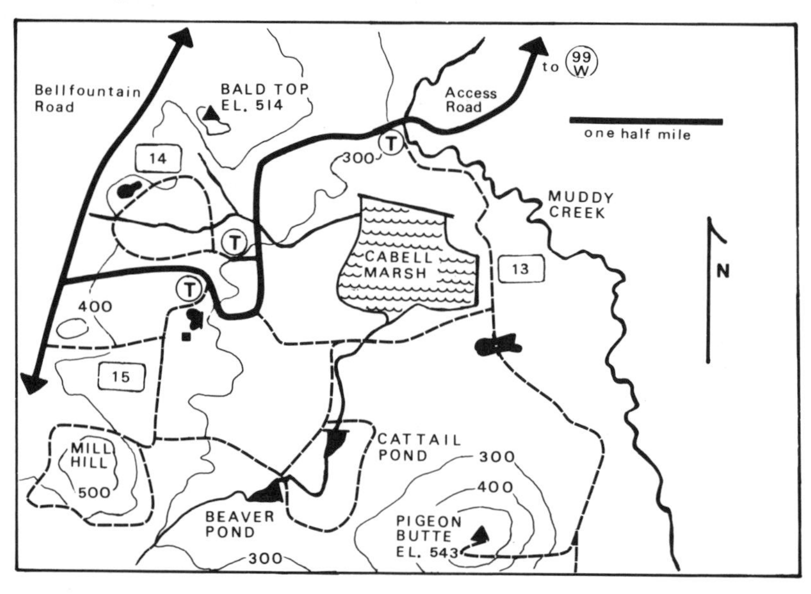

Muddy Creek to Pigeon Butte Trail

To reach the refuge from Corvallis, go 10 miles south on Oregon 99W, and turn west onto Finley Road at the sign. After 1.3 miles, turn south into the refuge. In .8 mile, there's a kiosk and comfort station. Brochures are generally available at the kiosk. The trailhead for Muddy Creek lies south, .4 mile beyond. Parking is on the right-hand side of the road, the trail is on the left.

The trail travels through ash woodland, tracing Muddy Creek and crossing a couple of bridges. Be quiet along this first stretch. It is here that the river otters can sometimes be seen romping over fallen branches or splashing in the water. Poison oak grows along the banks of Muddy Creek.

Camas, clover, and flowers from the pea family dot the tall grasses. Field mice burrow deep into the grassy shelter at the approach of the boot.

The trail then pulls away from the creek and travels through a cornfield (or stubble field, depending on season) to join an old road at .75 mile. Taking a left on the plant-embroidered road, the hiker soon arrives at Cabell Marsh. Here the swallows, red-winged blackbirds, wood ducks, and cinnamon teals engage with a flurry of wings and a discord of song. Animal paths lace the brushy border of the marsh. Nests abound.

At 1.1 miles, there's a junction. The trail to the right meets the Mill Hill–Ponds Loop Trail, Hike 15, in .5 mile. The trail straight ahead leads to Pigeon Butte.

At the junction at 1.9 miles, take a right uphill to Pigeon Butte. Beautiful twisted oaks, wild rose bushes, and wind-tossed grasses grace its back. Soon the hiker arrives at an old quarry site. This elevated perch provides a commanding view of the refuge, the tree-fringed course of Muddy Creek, and the surrounding farmland.

In the springtime, larkspur and dwarf star tulip lend delicate accents to the summit. Late-summer hikers must contend with the clinging affections of the dried grass seed.

From the quarry site the trail continues west, rounds the slope and climbs to the oak woodland atop Pigeon Butte at 2.3 miles.

The summit edge above the quarry is unstable, so be careful. Return as you came.

14 WOODPECKER LOOP

Distance: 1.2 miles round trip
Elevation Change: 100 feet
Difficulty: Easy
Map: Willamette Valley National Wildlife Refuges brochure
Water: Carry water
Season: All year
For More Information: William L. Finley National Wildlife Refuge

See map on page 58.

Hills, streams, marshes, and farmlands make up William L. Finley National Wildlife Refuge. Purchased with duck stamp monies, this 5325-acre refuge, along with the Baskett Slough and Ankeny refuges, provides a protected wintering habitat for dusky Canada geese.

The refuge is named for William L. Finley, the early-day naturalist who encouraged President Theodore Roosevelt to set aside such lands for wildlife protection.

In its 1.2 miles, Woodpecker Loop demonstrates the diversity of plant and animal life found in the transition zone of the Coast Range and the Willamette Valley. Here, five different species of woodpecker find suitable habitat, hence the trail's name. As the original name of the trail, "Poison Oak Loop," had equal appropriateness, it's wise to use caution when straying from the trail.

To reach the refuge from Corvallis, travel 10 miles south on Oregon 99W and turn west onto Finley Road at the sign. After

Woodpecker Loop

1.3 miles, turn south and travel .8 mile to a comfort station and a kiosk with a map display and refuge pamphlets. Another 1.5 miles beyond the kiosk, the road to the right leads to trailhead parking. This trail is open year-round.

Microenvironments of oak savanna, ash swale, mixed deciduous forest, and marsh add beauty to this wide gravel trail. The trail branches at .1 mile; tour the loop in either direction. Bridges and duckboards add charm and aid in the creek and marsh crossings.

The pond is a popular gathering area. Here, visitors pause to search the waters for life, while enjoying the tranquility of the setting. In springtime, a population of breeding newts occupies the pond. By late summer, most of the water has evaporated, leaving a mud hole dotted with the watchful eyes of submerged bullfrogs.

An array of birdhouses occupies the nearby trees. Some 212 bird species have been observed on the refuge. Binoculars and bird identification guides will enhance a stay.

The observation deck, shaded by a large oak, offers educational signboards and overlooks of the refuge. The shortness and ease of this trail invite leisurely investigation of all its offerings.

15 MILL HILL AND PONDS LOOPS

Distance: 4.6 miles
Elevation Change: 100 feet
Difficulty: Easy
Maps: USGS Monroe (unnecessary); Willamette Valley National Wildlife Refuges brochure
Water: Carry water
Season: May through October (with the Mill Hill portion open year-round)
For More Information: William L. Finley National Wildlife Refuge

See map on page 58.

William L. Finley National Wildlife Refuge is part of the greater Willamette Valley refuge complex for wintering duskies, a subspecies of Canada geese. Oak woodlands, mixed forests, meadows, marshes, ponds, and farmland create habitat diversity for the migrating and resident waterfowl and shorebird populations. Some 212 bird species have been identified at the refuge.

The Ponds Loop portion of this hike, like much of the refuge, is closed to visitors during the wintering season. This closure minimizes human disturbance to the birds, but some hunting is allowed in certain refuge zones.

In late spring–early summer, the microclimates of the refuge parade a rich variety of wildflowers. Iris, adder's tongue, dwarf star tulip, larkspur, and camass headline the attractions. Trails, with stretches of closed gravel road, conduct the discovery.

To reach the refuge from Corvallis, go 10 miles south on Oregon 99W, and take a right onto Finley Road. Go 1.3 miles, and turn south into the refuge. You'll come to a kiosk with a map display and brochures in .8 mile. From the kiosk, it is 1.8 miles south to the trailhead parking area, opposite the maintenance yard.

The trail begins at the wooden gate, at the west end of the wire-mesh fence. A mowed path guides the hiker around the closed area near the pond and maintenance yard. Swallows dart and glide, while low-flying hawks patrol the open field. Poison oak is abundant near the trail. In .3 mile, the trail merges with a gravel road.

At this point, an unmaintained .5-mile spur branches to the right. It dead ends at Bellfountain Road near milepost 10, after traveling the bush-lined path to an abandoned orchard.

The primary trail continues along the road, arriving at the Mill Hill Loop entrance in a short distance. Take a right for the trail, followed by another right at the fork, to begin a counterclockwise tour of the 1.5-mile loop. This introduces a mixed woodland, with many oaks and maples. An extraordinary number of galls litter

Birdhouse, William L. Finley National Wildlife Refuge

the path. Birds flit through the undergrowth but seldom reveal their identities.

Departing the woodland, the trail tours an open meadow of inviting grasses and wildflowers. Free from poison oak, the meadow is an engaging host. From the meadow, the trail travels the bench above Gray Creek Swamp, offering only glimpses of the wetland through the trees.

With the return to the road, the trail continues to the right. The road works its way along fields used during the winter by grazing geese. To the east rises Pigeon Butte, a refuge landmark. The next trail to the right tours Beaver and Cattail ponds. Stretches of this trail can become muddy.

Approaching the ponds, be quiet to avoid startling any wildlife. Occasionally, these ponds boil with leaping bullfrogs. Other times, the waters are calm as the moist-skinned residents placidly observe all through partially submerged eyes. Late summer finds the ponds reduced to mudholes with the resident bullfrogs still in place.

Departing the Cattail Pond area, the trail again comes to a road. Take a right to continue the loop. In .3 mile, there's a junction. Going right leads to the Muddy Creek–Pigeon Butte Trail, Hike 13. Going left returns to Finley Road in .3 mile. The trailhead parking area and the close of the loop lie .4 mile west of the trail's exit on Finley Road.

16 MARYS PEAK

Distance: 7.2 miles round trip (to observation point parking)
Elevation Change: 2300 feet
Difficulty: Strenuous
Maps: USGS Marys Peak; USFS Siuslaw National Forest
Water: Carry water
Season: Spring through fall
For More Information: Alsea Ranger District

The trail winds its way up the north slope of Marys Peak through coastal Douglas fir to the noble fir stands of the Marys Peak Scenic Botanical Area. In 1980, with this protective designation, the Forest Service acknowledged the value of the peak's botanic features and the need to perpetuate that value. At places, the mountainside rises at a 50-degree angle, but the design of the trail minimizes the steepness. Rustic benches along the way welcome the weary.

In its 2300-foot elevation gain, the trail tours a variety of microclimates: the second-growth Douglas fir forest at trail start, the hemlock-choked forest of mid-trail, the mature forest nearing the crest, and ultimately the open meadow of the summit.

Winter often brings snow to Marys Peak (elevation 4097 feet). Springtime is the favorite time to visit here, as the summit parades its wildflower colors and the clear, brisk days offer exceptional long-distance viewing.

From the junction of U.S. 20 and Oregon 34 west of Philomath, hikers take U.S. 20 west 1.7 miles, turning left onto Woods Creek

Wild ginger, Marys Peak Trail, Marys Peak

Road (Forest SR 2005). In 7.5 miles, the parking area for the Marys Peak Trail is found on the left, just before the gate.

For a shuttle hike or alternate approach to the trail from Oregon 34, hikers go 10 miles west of Philomath or 8.5 miles east of Alsea, turning north onto Marys Peak Road. The observation point parking lot is in 9.6 miles. The trail leaves from the northwest side of the lot, near the main road's entry point.

From the Woods Creek parking area, walk up the road, past the gate, to the trailhead. The trail uphill to the right leads to the observation point parking area and the summit (in 3.6 miles and 4.2 miles, respectively). The trail departing to the left is the Old Peak Road Trail (4 miles round trip).

The Old Peak Road Trail presently bears the intrusion of a neighboring clearcut, with notices of still other timber sales blazing the trees trailside. But once through the clearcut obstacle, this trail segment offers the greater reward with its vine maple archways, plentiful and varied undergrowth, and healthy, towering firs. It's ironic that the bounty that recommends this trail

Daisies atop Marys Peak

should also recommend its progressive destruction.

Looking to the trail's future, reforestation dollars have been set aside for rebuilding the trail, which will be completed in summer 1989. And, according to the Alsea District office, future sales, if any, will carry a similar provision. But the trail will display a much altered face.

The trail to the Marys Peak Observation Point, on the other hand, continues to offer unobstructed passage. The entry to this trail beckons with a lush groundcover similar to that found on the Old Peak Road Trail. Mats of oxalis, tangles of salal, and fountains of fern adorn the forest. Old-growth stumps and downed alders alone interrupt the greenery. Woods Creek rushes in the distance.

At .3 mile, the trail crosses a forest road, bidding farewell to this bounty. From here, the trail breaks into its climbing mode.

On hot summer days, the trail woos the hiker with shady passage. But there is a price for this comfort. In the hemlock-choked forest dominating the 1.2-mile stretch of trail above the forest road, the ground is barren—absent of visual diversity.

At 1.5 miles, that changes as the forest again opens up with large firs and fewer, younger hemlocks. Vanilla leaf, sword fern, and salal dispel the trancelike state brought on by the previous forest sameness.

At 2.4 miles, a small blue marker signals the arrival at the Marys Peak Scenic Botanical Area. Again, the plant community gains variety and abundance.

Before arriving at the northwest end of the parking lot, the trail traces a course below the road through meadow and forest. Springtime finds the meadow in its wildflower calico. In summer, the wind-bowed grasses invite a supine appreciation.

Arriving at the parking area, the hiker can proceed onward to the summit via the service road (.6 mile) or enjoy a picnic lunch and survey the setting. Clear days promise heart-thumping views

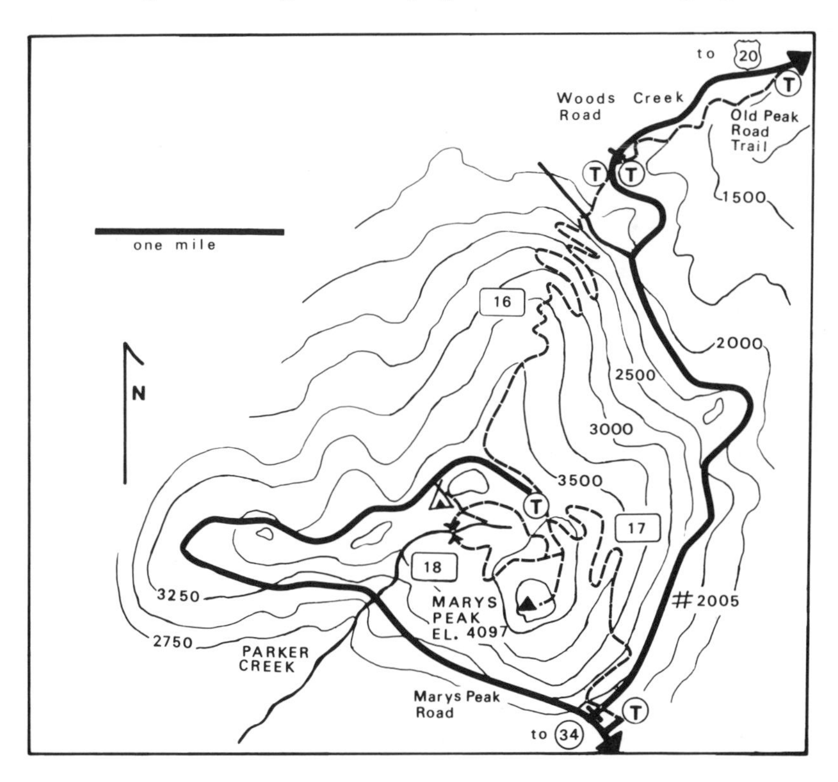

of the Cascade skyline featuring Mt. Washington, Mt. Jefferson, and Mt. Hood, with Mt. Adams, Mt. Saint Helens, and Mt. Rainier in the distance.

Return the way you came.

17 EAST RIDGE

Distance: 4.6 miles round trip
Elevation Change: 1100 feet
Difficulty: Moderate
Maps: USGS Marys Peak; USFS Siuslaw National Forest
Water: Carry water
Season: All year (in winter, call about road conditions and snow)
For More Information: Alsea Ranger District

See map on page 67.

Completed in 1985, the Marys Peak East Ridge Trail guides the visitor through a variety of vegetation types. The early part of the trail introduces a recovering clearcut with red currant, thimbleberry, salal, Oregon grape, and young Douglas fir. As the trail pulls up and away from Woods Creek Road, a mature forest of tall Douglas fir greets the hiker. Noble firs intermix with Douglas fir near the crest of Marys Peak, and in the summit meadows and along the crestline trail, mountain meadow plant species raise their heads.

The crest affords vistas of the Cascades and Willamette Valley. When fog fills the valley, Marys Peak seems an isolated island in a foamy sea.

In winter and early spring, snows are common to Marys Peak, and the upper levels of this trail promise a wintry treat.

On Oregon 34, 10 miles west of Philomath or 8.5 miles east of Alsea, hikers turn north onto Marys Peak Road and continue 5.5 miles. Trailhead parking is on the right (just before gated Woods Creek Road, Forest SR 2005). A second trailhead is found at the observation point parking area.

Beginning from the East Ridge trailhead, the trail angles down from the north side of the parking area. A sign marks its start. It then works its way through the brushy tangle of an old clearcut to cross Woods Creek Road (the watershed road) at .1 mile. In the young Douglas fir and salal, chickadees and juncos dart between branch and bush.

Soon the trail enters a mature forest. The forest floor shows little groundcover. The few fern and Oregon grape that grace the hillside accentuate the barrenness. But the straight, tall firs up the slope draw the eye skyward.

The trail steadily climbs. At 1 mile, East Ridge Trail makes its first switchback, sweeping southwest. Another switchback, and the hiker is again heading north. This trail lacks the familiar leaf or needle mat of other Coast Range trails.

The distant drumming of a grouse or an irritated challenge from a western gray squirrel alone interrupt the hiker's musings.

In another mile, the trail enters a long switchback, where meadowland and noble firs collide. Fairy slipper, yarrow, and lupine dot the meadow grasses. Sounds from the observation point replace the stillness. At 2.3 miles, the trail intersects the Marys Peak Trail (a gravel service road leading to the summit).

Going left on the Marys Peak Trail brings the hiker to the summit in .6 mile, or to the Meadow Edge Trail in .3 mile (Hike 18). Going right leads to the parking area and to the Marys Peak Trail, Hike 16.

Oregon Iris

View east from the East Ridge Trail, Marys Peak

Views from the crest of Marys Peak include the Cascades, featuring Mt. Jefferson and Mt. Hood; the Willamette Valley; Corvallis; and the ridges of the Coast Range. The summit vantage point extends the panorama with additional views to the west, including the Alsea River Valley.

Return as you came.

18 SUMMIT-MEADOW EDGE

Distance: 3.2 miles round trip
Elevation Change: 400 feet
Difficulty: Easy
Maps: USGS Marys Peak; USFS Siuslaw National Forest
Water: Parker Creek
Season: Spring through fall
For More Information: Alsea Ranger District

See map on page 67.

Marys Peak (elevation 4097 feet) is the highest point in the Coast Range. The summit beckons with its 360-degree view. North-south views of the Willamette Valley extend from Salem to Eugene. In the east looms the Cascade Range with its key features: Mt. Hood, Mt. Jefferson, Mt. Washington, Three-fingered Jack, the Three Sisters, and Bachelor Butte. Clear days add Mt. Adams, Mt. Saint Helens, and Mt. Rainier to the all-star lineup. The western horizon holds the rolling outline of the Coast Range and the Alsea River Valley.

The Meadow Edge Trail introduces the hiker to the noble fir stand of the Marys Peak Scenic Botanical Area (a Forest Service designation recognizing the botanical value of Marys Peak and ensuring protective management of the area). In the higher elevations, the forest presents an unadorned face, but as the trail winds down to Parker Creek, it sheds its plain image with accents of oxalis, bleeding heart, twisted stalk, and vanilla leaf. Mountain meadows of wind-tossed, waist-high grasses bridge the forest segments of the trail.

View of Alsea River Valley from Marys Peak summit

Meadow profusion, Marys Peak

On Oregon 34, 10 miles west of Philomath or 8.5 miles east of Alsea, turn north onto Marys Peak Road. Trailhead parking is at the observation point parking lot in 9.6 miles.

The trail begins on the gravel service road, north of the comfort station. In .3 mile, the Meadow Edge Trail departs to the right. The summit lies at the end of the gravel road in another .3 mile.

There's an electronic communications site on the summit, but an open meadow welcomes a blanket and a picnic lunch. Every direction competes for the visitor's attention. The view is ever changing with the hour of the day and with the season. Repeat visits bring new rewards.

From the junction at .3 mile, the Meadow Edge Trail quickly disappears into the noble fir forest. At the entrance to the trail, the early-morning visitor may surprise a deer basking in the meadow, with the safety of the forest immediately to its back. Swallows sweep the sky.

The trail is well marked with legends and map boards. In 100 yards, the trail splits, forming a loop. Traveling clockwise, the hiker is greeted by a thriving canopy of firs contrasted by a barren slope. Only a few stout plants pierce the void. But the firs are commanding performers.

The wind whistles and lashes at the tree tops, but the hiker is mostly protected from its ire. Leaving the shelter of the forest, the trail snakes through a meadow of waist-high grasses, laced with bracken fern, lupine, and yarrow.

In the distance, the mill in Toledo coughs up puffy white billows. Clearcuts patchwork the neighboring hillsides. At .5 mile (distance measured from the loop's start), the trail cuts back into the forest. As it descends the slope, the variety and abundance of groundcover increase. Rounding the bend at .8 mile, the trail showcases a beautiful green slope punctuated with tall, straight noble fir. The serenity of the setting slows the hiker's stride.

An old-growth stump announces the Parker Creek bridge. Monkey flowers, ferns, salmonberry, and a profusion of water-loving plants makes this riparian environment a trail highlight.

Exiting the bridge, the trail turns right. Fireweed, thistle, columbine, and daisy color the former roadbed, while thimbleberry, salmonberry, and alder soften its edges. At 1.1 miles, the trail continues straight. Side trails branch to Parker Creek (right) and to the campground (left). Nettles grow along the creek.

At 1.5 miles, the trail returns to the meadow edge.

In .4 mile, the loop closes, and in another 100 yards the Meadow Edge Trail converges with the Summit Trail. Go left to find the parking area in .3 mile. Go right to return to the summit for another look.

19 HORSE CREEK (NORTH)

Distance: 7.6 miles round trip (6.7 miles with Harris Ranch loop option)
Elevation Change: 800 feet
Difficulty: Moderate
Maps: USGS Tidewater; USFS Siuslaw National Forest
Water: Drift Creek
Season: All year
For More Information: Waldport Ranger District

This 5800-acre wilderness area offers the floral wealth and diversity of an old-growth forest and the beauty of Drift Creek. Douglas fir and western hemlock dominate the woodland, with Sitka spruce and cedar growing in the moist areas. Red alder and bigleaf maple reign creekside, and everywhere cascading greenery dresses the forest floor.

In 1979, Drift Creek was designated a roadless area, and in 1984 that designation was upgraded to wilderness area. Prior to 1979, forest management practices marked the area as primitive—not for development.

The trail bears the unlikely name "Horse Creek Trail," as it is a fragment of the old forest management trail of that name, which

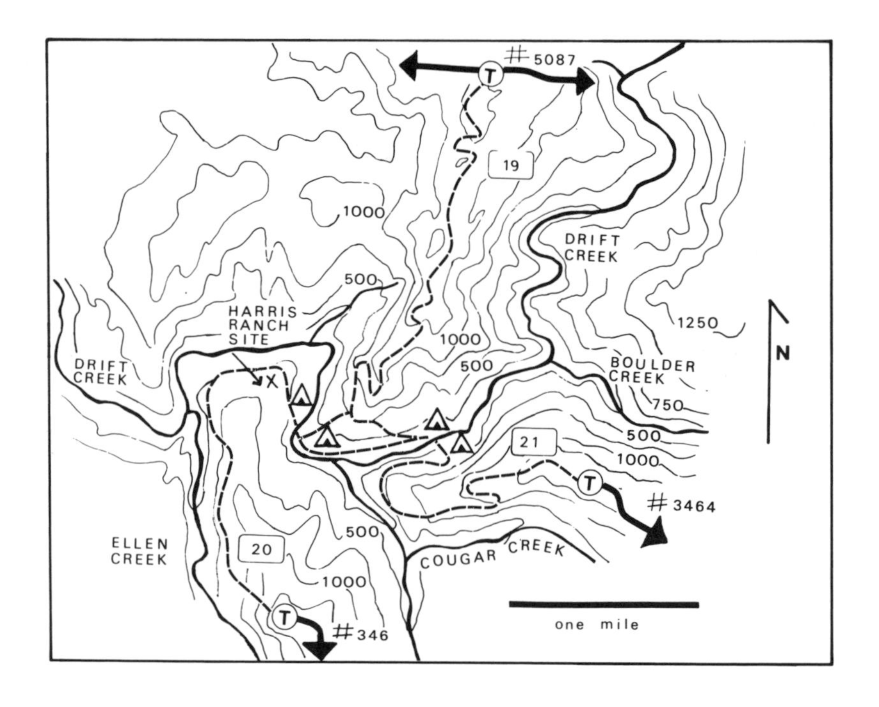

ran between the Toledo and Tidewater quadrangles. The normally driving waters of Drift Creek isolate the northern section of Horse Creek Trail from its southern companion, Hike 21. Only during late summer does Drift Creek permit fording to join these two trails.

From U.S. 101 near Ona Beach State Park, turn east onto North Beaver Creek Road (County 602). Immediately following the Beaver Creek crossing, in 3.8 miles, turn right onto North Elkhorn Road (Forest SR 51).

In 5.8 miles, Forest SR 51 comes to a T. Going left on Forest SR 50 for 1.3 miles leads to a sign for the Horse Creek Trail. A right turn onto Forest SR 5087 leads to the pavement's end, but the good graded surface is easily passable for conventional vehicles. Trailhead parking is to the left in 3.4 miles. The trailhead is marked.

The trail begins ascending the roadside slope before turning inland to the wilderness. For the first mile, the trail assumes an even grade, working its way along a ridge. But the thick forest prohibits vistas.

A scattering of red cedar accents this stand of Douglas fir and western hemlock, while salal, Oregon grape, and sword fern drape the forest floor. Where the hemlock gains dominance, the understory thins.

Despite the frequent, heavy rains of winter, the ground is remarkably absorbent and free from erosion. For hiking in the rain, this trail affords great comfort. The thick canopy deflects the force of the rain, and the trail, absent of puddles, invites carefree hiking. Rain showers also present the old-growth forest in its finery, with shimmering leaves and raindrop jewels.

Elk usage of the trail shows in the breaking away of the soft shoulders and occasional ruptures in the trailbed itself. But the impact is slight compared with the reward of the presence of elk.

Between .7 mile and 1 mile, salmonberry crowds the trail. Hereafter, the plant is encountered off and on, primarily on the open slopes.

At 1.2 miles, the trail abandons its even course along the ridge's east side to zigzag down the south flank. The switchbacks are well designed to slow descent, without introducing tiresome, unnecessary distance.

At 1.8 miles the alders begin to appear, and at 2.5 miles an unmaintained side trail departs to the right. This spur meets the north end of the Harris Ranch Trail in .4 mile. It's steep but easy to follow, and it allows the hiker to add a loop to the close of the hike.

On the main trail, at 3 miles, the hiker arrives at a junction. To the left lies a creekside camp and the end of Horse Creek (North).

Drift Creek in late summer

From the opposite shore, the sign for Horse Creek (South) beckons the late summer hiker.

A right at the junction introduces the north segment of the Harris Ranch Trail, a flat trail paralleling the creek. Alder, bigleaf maple, and salmonberry dominate a landscape dashed with cedar and hemlock. At .7 mile, the trail passes a grassy bench, and in another 100 yards the trail ends at Drift Creek.

When low water permits fording, the hike may be extended with a tour of the southern portion of the Harris Ranch Trail, Hike 20.

From the end of Harris Ranch (North), the spur to the right leads to some prime campsites, a short distance up the trail. Following the unmaintained path uphill from here, .4 mile brings the hiker back to Horse Creek (North), as mentioned earlier, putting a loop on the end of the hike.

Forgoing the unmaintained spur, return the way you came.

20 HARRIS RANCH

Distance: 5 miles round trip
Elevation Change: 1100 feet
Difficulty: Moderate
Maps: USGS Tidewater; USFS Siuslaw National Forest
Water: Drift Creek
Season: All year
For More Information: Waldport Ranger District

See map on page 74.

The Harris Ranch Trail introduces the hiker to a lush old-growth environment, a delicate meadowland, and the coursing waters of Drift Creek. The old growth is predominantly Douglas fir and western hemlock, dotted with western red cedar and Sitka spruce. Lichen and moss adorn the trunks and arms of the bigleaf maples and alders that grow in the moister regions.

The meadowland is bordered by trailing blackberry and is thick with grasses and ferns. Its soft, marshy ground long remembers the tread of a boot.

The meadow is a popular area for deer and elk, and the clear waters of Drift Creek are always a draw, supporting wild runs of steelhead, and chinook and coho salmon, as well as the resident population of crayfish and trout. Dippers dive and bob in the chill waters.

The last party to occupy this land was the Harris family. To the locals, the property was familiarly called "the Harris Place." But the trail manager felt that designation inappropriate, and the trail was christened Harris Ranch.

To reach this trail from the junction of U.S. 101 and Oregon 34 in Waldport, head east on Oregon 34 for 7.3 miles. After crossing over the Alsea River, take a left on Risley Creek Road (Forest SR 3446) and go another 4.1 miles. A sign for the Harris Ranch Trail indicates a left turn onto Forest SR 346. Go .7 mile and turn off Forest SR 346. The trailhead is found at the end of the road (.3 mile). Although the roads are either paved or good graded dirt surfaces, parts of the parking area can become muddy.

Campsite, Drift Creek Wilderness

From the well-marked trailhead, the hiker is immediately immersed in old-growth splendor. The senses are bombarded with stimuli: color, texture and shape, shadow and light, a cool dampness, and the intermingling smell of life and decay. Hemlock and fir, salal and ferns vie for real estate.

Unlike Hike 19, Horse Creek (North), this trail seems to have great purpose as it marches down the slope, with steep sections. Between 1 and 1.3 miles, the trail temporarily flattens, but again resumes its downward intent. Mosses soften the trail's edge.

At 2.1 miles, it arrives at a meadow. Here, and along the trail immediately preceding the meadow, tracks and flattened foliage announce the presence of deer and elk.

To the right of where the trail enters the meadow, the hiker discovers the time-touched chimney of the old Harris place, secluded in the alders. Blackberry streamers, ferns, and moss ornament its stone face. Nettles challenge closer viewing.

Several footpaths depart from the meadow's south boundary. Harris Ranch Trail branches to the right.

The meadow itself invites low-impact camping, but the more responsible camper will continue on the path straight ahead to three or four beautiful campsites along the creek. The exposed bedrock near shore invites sunseeker and the angler.

Continuing along Harris Ranch Trail, at 2.5 miles the hiker again arrives at the Drift Creek shore. On the opposite bank rests the northern segment of this trail and Horse Creek (North), Hike 19. But the usually deep, fast waters of Drift Creek prohibit fording, except in late summer.

Return the way you came. The discovery can be extended, though, by following the faint outline of an old wagon road journeying west from the meadow.

21 HORSE CREEK (SOUTH)

Distance: 4.5 miles round trip
Elevation Change: 1200 feet
Difficulty: Moderate
Maps: USGS Tidewater; USFS Siuslaw National Forest
Water: Drift Creek
Season: All year
For More Information: Waldport Ranger District

See map on page 74.

Drift Creek Wilderness seduces the hiker with its tranquil old-growth forest and the rushing beauty of Drift Creek. The lush multiple-story old growth is an orchestration of texture, shape, color, and lighting. While the plants are familiar—Oregon grape, salal, fern, salmonberry, and oxalis—it's their union and abun-

Passing a quiet moment beside Drift Creek

Skunk cabbage

dance under the old-growth canopy that renders them uncommon. The rich and varied plant life draping the water's edge further adds to the enchantment.

The area received wilderness protection in 1984. The unlikely name of "Horse Creek Trail" traces back to the original, more extensive forest management trail of that name, which incorporated this segment.

For the greater portion of the hiking season, this is an isolated trail. But for a few months in late summer, the water level of Drift Creek permits the trail's linkage with Horse Creek (North), Hike 19.

Beginning from the junction of U.S. 101 and Oregon 34 in Waldport, head east on Oregon 34 for 7.3 miles. After crossing over the Alsea River, take a left onto Risley Creek Road (Forest SR 3446) and travel another 7.3 miles. A sign for the Horse Creek Trail indicates a left turn onto Forest SR 3464. The trailhead lies at the end of the road in 1.6 miles.

Each of the three trails exploring the Drift Creek Wilderness (Hikes 19, 20, 21) possesses a different character and offers a different window on the wilderness. This trail's leisurely, winding nature provides a "Sunday drive" introduction to the old-growth forest of Douglas fir and western hemlock. Each step draws the hiker steadily downward toward the creek.

In the springtime, the salmonberry blooms emit a rich, heady smell that envelops the trail. Likewise in the spring, the small drainages along the trail's second half announce themselves with the strong aroma of the resident skunk cabbage. Always, the greenery soothes the eye and the spirit.

At 2.25 miles, the trail arrives at the shoreline of Drift Creek. Following the angler's trail that departs to the right .1 mile leads to a large tree-sheltered campsite. The trail briefly fades, but by continuing in its general direction the hiker can easily relocate the trampled path.

An occasional dipper strafes the surface of Drift Creek. And in the isolated ponds and creek shallows bypassed by this angler's trail, crayfish speed to safety beneath the rocks.

Maianthemum, bleeding heart, oxalis, sword fern, and Oregon grape crowd the banks of the creek, with maples and alders reigning overhead. Moss-covered rocks interrupting the water's course add to the Drift Creek charm.

The face of Drift Creek is greatly altered with the passage of the seasons, as the power of winter bows to the sleepy calm of summer. When water levels permit fording, care is advised.

Return the way you came.

22 GIANT SPRUCE-CAPE PERPETUA VIEWPOINT

Distance: 5 miles round trip
Elevation Change: 600 feet
Difficulty: Moderate
Maps: USGS Waldport; USFS Siuslaw National Forest
Water: Available at Visitor Center
Season: All year
For More Information: Cape Perpetua Visitor Center or Waldport Ranger District

This loop travels three of the Cape Perpetua System trails: Giant Spruce, St. Perpetua, and Whispering Spruce Loop. Highlights include a 500-year-old Sitka spruce and the spectacular ocean and coastal vistas seen from Cape Perpetua. Cape Perpetua's giant spruce stands 190 feet high, since the Columbus Day Storm of 1962 stole 30 feet from its top. The quiet beauty of Cape Creek is an added attraction along the forest trail.

Whispering Spruce Loop, the trail segment atop the headland, boasts a view encompassing the 150-mile expanse bounded by Cape Foulweather to the north and Cape Blanco to the south. Its stone structures—Parapet (formerly called South View Point) and

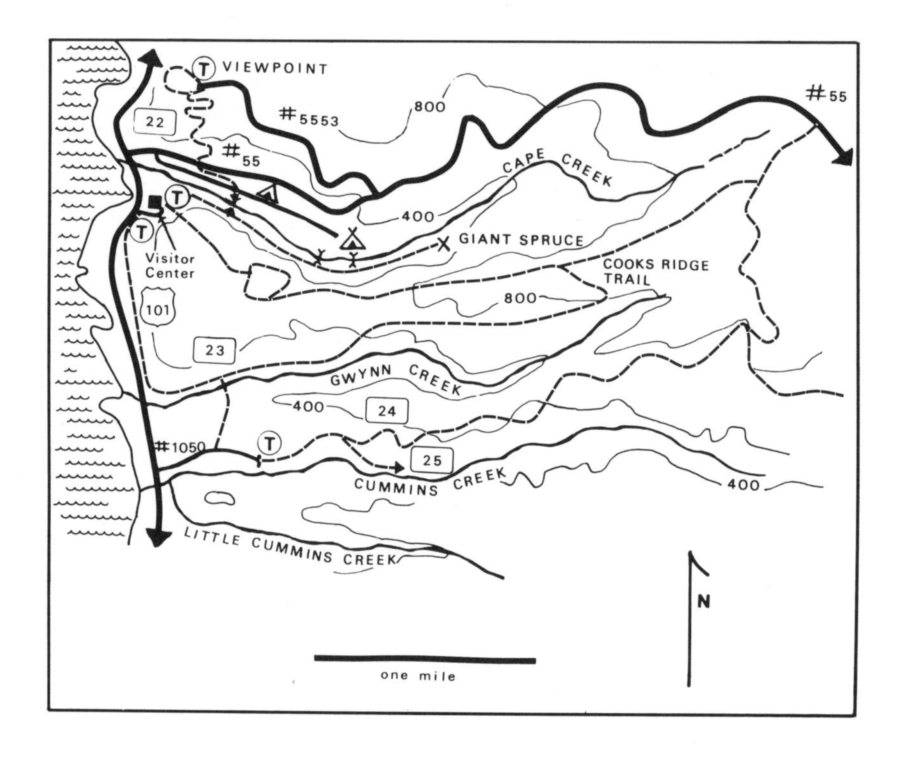

Coastline viewed from South Parapet

West Shelter, Whispering Spruce Loop

West Shelter, built by the Civilian Conservation Corps (the CCC) in 1938—today serve as scenic outposts for ocean viewing and whalewatching.

First sighted on March 7, 1778, Cape Perpetua received its name from Captain James Cook. There are two theories regarding the origin of the name. The first relates to the discovery date, March 7, the date of St. Perpetua's martyrdom in 203 A.D. The second comes from Captain Cook's journal entry noting his storm-prolonged stay and the ever-present headland.

Two trailheads serve this trail. One is located at the Cape Perpetua Visitor Center (3 miles south of Yachats on the east side of U.S. 101).

The second lies at the Cape Perpetua Viewpoint off Forest SR 55. On U.S. 101, travel .3 mile north from the Cape Perpetua Visitor Center, turn east onto Forest SR 55, and follow the signs to the viewpoint.

From the northeast corner of the visitor center entryway, the Giant Spruce Trail departs. As it drops away from the visitor center, salal, thimbleberry, huckleberry, and salmonberry form its border. In the fall, this trail hosts "berry walks" conducted by naturalists.

Springtime finds the trail well-trodden by elk, which feed on the tender young shoots growing along Cape Creek. Ferns, bleeding heart, trillium, oxalis, and *Maianthemum,* or wild lily of the valley, thrive in this moist environment.

At the trail junction in .2 mile, the trail to the viewpoint and campground departs to the left. This is the first of several spurs linking the campground to the Giant Spruce Trail.

Remaining on the Giant Spruce Trail, the hiker crosses several side creeks. Colossal-leafed skunk cabbages crowd the moist hollows. Their pungent perfume tangs the spring air.

Larger Sitkas characterize the forest, just prior to the arrival at Giant Spruce (.9 mile). A bench and a stairway encircling the featured attraction facilitate a better acquaintance. The hole at the giant's base indicates that it was nurtured by a nurse tree.

When ready to trade views of the forest for views of the ocean, retrace the Giant Spruce Trail to the Cape Viewpoint Trail junction. Taking a right leads to a scenic bridge over the bubbling clear waters of Cape Creek. Greenery abounds creekside. Salmonberry and alder prosper.

Enter the campground, and angle left across the grounds to regain the trail near the pay station.

The trail then crosses Forest SR 55 and begins its ascent of the St. Perpetua Trail. An open Sitka spruce forest, with fir and hemlock interspersed, houses the trail. Sword and deer fern, salal, and huckleberry gain a stronghold trailside.

Leaving the forest, the trail then zigzags up the cape's grass-covered south face to the St. Perpetua–Whispering Spruce trail junction.

A left on Whispering Spruce leads the hiker to the loop's Parapet. Heceta Head Lighthouse, Cummins Ridge, and the contemporary-looking Cape Perpetua Visitor Center add to the view to the south. During whalewatching season (late fall to early spring), this is a popular post at which to raise binoculars and scopes.

The .3-mile loop takes the hiker along the ridge, past West Shelter, and through an alder thicket (formerly cleared for a World War II artillery installation), before it exits at the parking lot. In recent years, the loop trail has also served as a movie set.

From the parking area, re-enter the loop, returning to the Whispering Spruce–St. Perpetua trail junction. Taking a left on the St. Perpetua Trail returns the hiker to the visitor center.

23 GWYNN CREEK-COOKS RIDGE LOOP

Distance: 5.4 miles or 6 miles with the Riggin Slinger Loop
Elevation Change: 1100 feet
Difficulty: Moderate
Maps: USGS Waldport; USFS Siuslaw National Forest
Water: Intermittent side creeks
Season: All year
For More Information: Cape Perpetua Visitor Center or Waldport Ranger District

See map on page 74.

Introducing this hike, the Oregon Coast Trail component of Gwynn Creek Trail traces a length of the original wagon road that ran between Yachats and Florence. Built in 1895, the wagon road was used until 1910. Today, tightly bunched Sitka spruce usher the hiker along the route.

Turning inland the trail exchanges ocean vistas for coastal old-growth habitat and views of Gwynn Creek Canyon. The muffled sound of the ocean, the rippling waters of Gwynn Creek, and the rush of the wind are the hiker's companions.

The coastline is subject to storms and heavy winds. Like much of the state, this area was punished by the Columbus Day Storm of 1962. Cooks Ridge bears the badge of that storm in the area recovering from the follow-up salvage cut and burn of 1965.

Prior to Captain Cook's discovery of Cape Perpetua, the Indians occupied this area, harvesting shellfish and, according to legend, harvesting gold. In the 1900s, gold seekers acting on these stories set up sluices on nearby Cape Creek, but found little success.

The initial protection of Cape Perpetua began in 1949 with the designation of 500 acres. By 1979, the number of protected acres stood at 2000.

The Gwynn Creek trailhead is located on the south side of the Cape Perpetua Visitor Center driveway. The visitor center lies east off U.S. 101, about 3 miles south of Yachats or 11.7 miles north of Sea Lion Caves.

Parking is available at the visitor center, if you plan to complete the hike during the posted hours. The Visitor Center is scheduled to be open from 9:00 am to 5:00 pm daily throughout the year—budget permitting. Call ahead for current schedule. There's adequate turnout parking along U.S. 101 should your hours differ from those of the center.

Following the old wagon road, the trail begins tracing a bench above U.S. 101. Salmonberry, alder, and spruce dominate its border. At .7 mile, the trail turns inland. Soon afterward, the hiker arrives at the junction to the connector trail tying together the Gwynn Creek Trail and the Cummins Creek Trail, Hike 24.

Gwynn Creek-Cooks Ridge Loop Trail

Beyond the junction, the trail assumes an elevated course along Gwynn Creek's north bank. The narrow path of Gwynn Creek and its brushy canyon contrast with the rich, green Sitka spruce–hemlock forest that now characterizes the trail.

At 2 miles, the trail pulls away from the creek. As it begins to climb, more Douglas firs invade the forest complex. For a quarter mile, the trail tours a healing fire zone. In a half mile, the uphill character of the trail becomes more pronounced.

At the ridge crest is the T junction of the Cooks Ridge Trail. Going right on the Ridge Trail leads to the east end of the Cummins Creek Trail in 1.2 miles. Continuing left on Cooks Ridge takes the hiker to the visitor center and the close of this loop.

Completing the loop, the hiker reaches the highest point of the trail at 3.5 miles. From here, the character of the forest and groundcover undergoes abrupt changes from lush and fern-plentiful to open and dry. The forest is mainly second growth.

At 4.6 miles, the trail enters a stand of giant Sitka spruce interspersed with hemlock and crowded with fern. Through the branchwork, the hiker secures views of Cape Perpetua to the north.

Just ahead lies the Riggin Slinger Loop, a .6-mile former nature trail. In either direction, it's an enjoyable .3 mile to the Visitor Center Trail. At 5.4 miles, the hiker arrives at the visitor center and the close of the loop.

24 CUMMINS CREEK

Distance: 6.8 miles round trip or 7.4 miles forming the loop
Elevation Change: 1000 feet
Difficulty: Moderate
Maps: USGS Waldport; USFS Siuslaw National Forest
Water: Carry water (a few intermittent runoffs on loop)
Season: All year
For More Information: Cape Perpetua Visitor Center or Waldport Ranger District

See map on page 82.

The Cummins Creek Trail is a new addition to the Cape Perpetua Trail System. The 1985 land trade cleared the way for the Forest Service to close Forest SR 1050, giving birth to this trail. Because of its newness, nature has had little time to remodel its face, but the Cummins Creek Trail holds promise for the future.

Presently, it offers exceptional skyline viewing of the rich Douglas fir–Sitka spruce forests of Cape Perpetua and the Cummins Creek Wilderness. From the ridge, views of the ocean, Cummins Peak, Cummins Ridge, and the Cummins Creek drainage detain the hiker. But the hiker never approaches Cummins Creek. Its muffled voice can only be heard near the beginning of the trail.

Since the September 1985 release of the tansy ragwort flea beetle, the Cummins Creek Trail has also served as a biological research station. Tansy ragwort, a yellow flowering weed, is the nemesis of livestock growers across the country. And this tiny beetle feeds solely on this plant.

To reach Cummins Creek Trail from U.S. 101, hikers go south from the Cape Perpetua Visitor Center for 1.1 miles or north from Sea Lion Caves for 10.6 miles. A turn east onto Forest SR 1050 leads to trailhead parking in .3 mile.

The trail traces the shared boundary of the Cape Perpetua Scenic Area and the Cummins Creek Wilderness, offering views of each but not intimate acquaintances. At .2 mile, a side trail departs to the right, leading into the Cummins Creek Wilderness to arrive at Cummins Creek, Hike 25.

Game trails lace across the former road, disappearing into the forest. On these, the hiker can periodically duck into the trees to study the variety and texture of the forest floor and gain an appreciation of the forest denied by the road-trail.

At 2.3 miles, the Cummins Creek Trail takes a left up the time-touched logging road bordered by alders. This marks the beginning of a steady uphill. Alternatively, continuing straight from this point, along the road, the hiker can explore an additional .6 mile before arriving at a road closure and trail end.

Red-flowering Currant

The hill that the trail climbs was previously privately owned and clearcut, but sufficient time has passed to heal the scar on the land. Young evergreens, alders, shrubs, and grasses soften the cut's appearance. Lupine, salal, and red currant add springtime color.

In a quarter mile and again in another half mile, the hiker gains good ocean vistas and views of neighboring features in the Coast Range. From the ridge, the harsh appearance of recent clearcuts greets the hiker. The forest here has been extensively logged over the past 20 years. Plants along the ridge exhibit an alpinelike character, growing smaller and closer to the ground.

At 3.4 miles, the hiker arrives at the Cooks Ridge Trail junction. From here, the hiker can either return along the trail just walked or return via Cooks Ridge and Gwynn Creek trails (Hike 23) and the .3-mile connecting spur to complete a loop.

In taking the loop, most of the 1.2-mile distance traveled on Cooks Ridge is on exposed roadbed, bordered by recovering clearcuts, with the final quarter mile in open forest.

But the rich old-growth environment and scenic creek of the Gwynn Creek Trail (2.4 miles) make it an enjoyable loop.

From the connecting spur's exit onto Forest SR 1050, take a left to complete the loop and return to the vehicle.

25 CUMMINS CREEK WILDERNESS

Distance: 2.4 miles round trip
Elevation Change: 100 feet
Difficulty: Easy
Maps: USGS Waldport; USFS Siuslaw National Forest
Water: Cummins Creek
Season: All year
For More Information: Waldport Ranger District

This unmaintained trail assumes an elevated course along the north bank of Cummins Creek. Old-growth Sitka spruce, lush fern beds, and isolated meadows accent the trek, as Cummins Creek gurgles in the background. The branchwork maze charac-

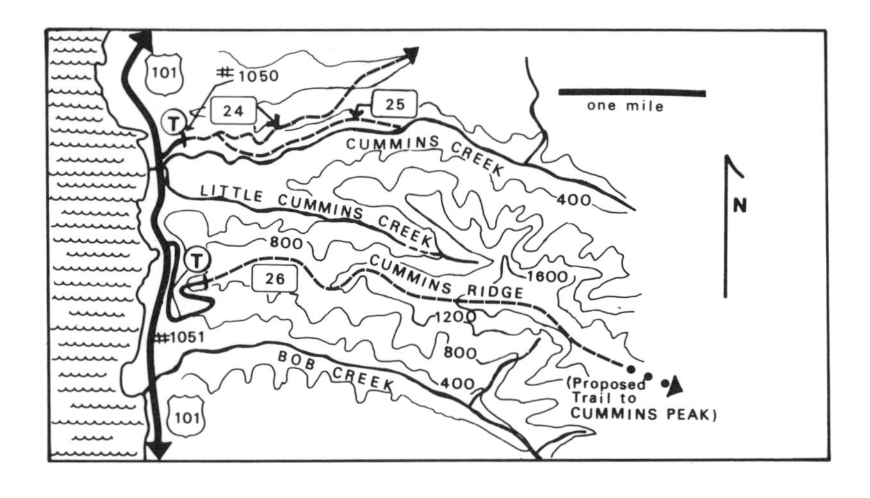

Cummins Creek

teristic of the Sitka spruce endows this trail with a restful quality—cool, shaded, and animated as the light plays through the branches.

The close of the trail brings the hiker to a clearing and the sparkling waters of Cummins Creek. The setting here preserves the tranquility found on the trail. Cummins Creek received wilderness protection under the 1984 Oregon Wilderness Bill.

With the trailhead easily accessed from U.S. 101, this trail makes a pleasant addition to an Oregon coast holiday. On U.S. 101, traveling south 1.1 miles from the Cape Perpetua Visitor Center or north 10.6 miles from Sea Lion Caves, turn east onto Forest SR 1050. Trailhead parking is at the road closure in .3 mile.

The trail shares its first .2 mile with the Cummins Creek Trail of the Cape Perpetua System, Hike 24, before departing south and entering the Cummins Creek Wilderness. An old road, softened by time, leads the way into the wilderness.

Within the next quarter mile, the old road dies, and the trail branches. The trail to the right leads to the creek in 100 yards. The trail straight ahead, the primary trail, stays inland, paralleling the course of Cummins Creek.

Old-growth Sitka spruce, hemlock, black huckleberry, horsetail reeds, trillium, and skunk cabbage provide a rich backdrop for the walk. Above and to the north, the hiker can see the Douglas fir towers of Cape Perpetua, and to the south the skyline of Cummins Ridge. In the late fall, mushroom collectors tour the trail with anticipation. Lichens hanging from the overhead branches filter the sunlight.

Although it is unmaintained, the trail is in excellent condition, save for a few marshy areas, which one can easily negotiate with the help of some well-placed logs and rocks..

At 1 mile, the trail's outline grows faint, but it remains easy to follow. There's an overgrown huckleberry bush and a few more downfallen branches here. But the trail again becomes clear, before concluding on the Cummins Creek shore at 1.2 miles.

Red alders and moss-draped maples overhang the creek, and the opposite bank hosts a fern-filled meadow. Cummins Creek represents yet another clear-water prize of the Coast Range and an invitation to linger.

26 CUMMINS RIDGE

Distance: 7 miles round trip (may be extended by traveling the flagged route cross-country, along the ridge to Cummins Peak)
Elevation Change: 600 feet
Difficulty: Moderate
Maps: USGS Waldport and Heceta Head; USFS Siuslaw National Forest
Water: Carry water
Season: All year
For More Information: Waldport Ranger District

See map on page 90.

The Cummins Ridge Trail itself is evidence of the battle for the Cummins Creek Wilderness: the push for road construction vs. the push for preservation. In this case, the wilderness won, and road construction was halted.

Time has softened the roadbed's appearance. Today, a flowing band of tall grasses, wildflowers, and young alders adorns the

Coastal fog in the Cummins Creek Wilderness

back of Cummins Ridge. Elk and deer trails weave across the roadbed, disappearing into the wilderness.

The north side of the trail offers limited views of Cape Perpetua and the Cummins Creek drainage.

In forthcoming years, as funding becomes available, the Forest Service plans to extend this trail from the road closure to Cummins Peak. In 1987, the trail manager flagged the route. When complete, this new trail segment will offer an additional 2.5 miles of discovery. In the meantime, the flagged trail invites cross-country travel.

An exploration of this burgeoning trail starts by taking U.S. 101 south .6 mile from Neptune State Park, followed by a turn east onto Forest SR 1051. A sign on U.S. 101 indicates the turn for the Cummins Ridge Trail. Travel 2 miles along this one-lane road to its closure and trailhead parking.

The trail begins tracing the south slope of the ridge, with a steady climb. Ushering the hiker along the ridge is the typical fir–spruce complex of the coast, with alders overtaking the clearings. Sword and bracken fern and salal make a healthy showing, spilling trailside. Tansy ragwort splashes the trail with vibrant yellow flowers.

Under full sun, the open trail can prove a scorcher. Carry plenty of water. More often, though, the trail's coastal location mitigates the heat with cooling breezes or masking fog.

At .3 mile, alders gain a stronghold. Already, these young trees promise to be the nemesis of the trail maintenance crew. Nearing the midway point, the trail rounds a bend and begins to descend.

On the final leg of the journey, the trail crosses over the ridge and travels the north slope. Trees filter views of Cape Perpetua and the Cummins Creek drainage. The trail halts at 3.5 miles, at the small rock barrier at the close of an alder-narrowed stretch of road.

Just prior to the road's entry into the second, uppermost clearcut unit, the newly flagged trail to Cummins Peak departs the road and journeys uphill, to the right. This cross-country trek delivers a better appreciation for the wilderness old growth.

Eventually, the Forest Service hopes to connect the Cummins Ridge Trail to the Cape Perpetua Trail System.

27 ROCK CREEK WILDERNESS

Distance: 2.2 miles round trip
Elevation Change: 100 feet
Difficulty: Easy
Maps: USGS Heceta Head; USFS Siuslaw National Forest
Water: Rock Creek; water available at campground
Season: All year
For More Information: Waldport Ranger District

On August 11, 1984, beneath the apple tree in the homestead meadow, the Forest Service formally dedicated Rock Creek and Cummins Creek wildernesses. The homestead, last owned by the Bowman family, was abandoned some 40 years ago. The Forest Service acquired the land in 1966.

Rock Creek

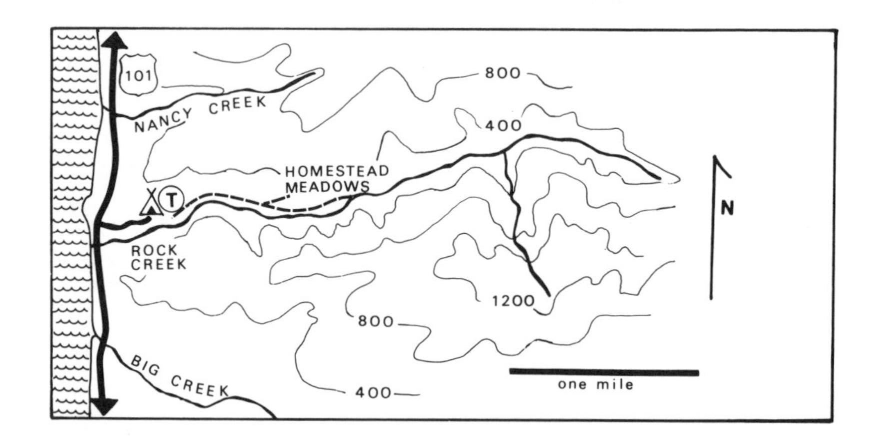

The old-growth forest of Rock Creek Wilderness lends a rich texture to the canyon and creates a vital watershed. Its canopy provides an unlikely nesting habitat for the marbled murrelet, a seabird.

Billed as a fisherman's path, the unmaintained trail to the homestead meadows is the only hiker access to this 7400-acre wilderness, and the Forest Service has no plans for trail development. The greatest resource value of this area is its wildlife. With prime feeding and birthing sites here, wildlife advancement supersedes recreational pursuits.

The trail traces the old homestead road, which is now largely reclaimed by middle- and lower-story plants and bushes. Deer and elk range the area. The meadows' marshy areas support salamanders and frogs. The clear waters of Rock Creek entice both fisherman and poet.

The natural meadows between Rock Creek Wilderness and the ocean represent an important hatching ground for the endangered silver spot butterfly.

To reach Rock Creek Wilderness from U.S. 101, drive 4.8 miles north of Sea Lion Caves or 6.9 miles south of the Cape Perpetua Visitor Center. Rock Creek Forest Service Campground is on the east side of U.S. 101. There is no hiker parking within the campground; use the turnouts on U.S. 101 and hike to the campground trailhead (.4 mile).

The trail leaves from the east-end campsite and assumes a course slightly inland from Rock Creek's north bank. Although unmaintained, the trail is quite wide and pleasantly free from slapping bushes. Obstacles are few, namely some downfalls to step over and some marshy drainages.

Oxalis, *Maianthemum,* horsetail reeds, salmonberry, blackberry, red currant, and alder provide the trailside adornment.

The first .3 mile is well--tracked and easily traveled. At .3 mile, the trail forks. The upper fork, to the left, takes the hiker to the smaller upper meadows in .1 mile. The area along the small side creek can become muddy. Passage requires boots or a carefree attitude.

From the upper meadows, the hiker gains an overview of the lower meadow and Rock Creek. A webwork of secondary trails riddles the forest above the meadows.

Taking a right at the .3-mile junction leads to the lower meadow. Where the trail appears to end at the bushes, a cut to the right crosses over the small side creek. The trail now draws closer to the north bank of Rock Creek, and in 100 yards the hiker enters the homestead meadow from its southwest corner.

It's a long east-west meadow stretching nearly .2 mile. A couple of apple trees, some fence posts, and some old bottles remain from the homestead years. In the springtime, yellow skunk cabbage freckles the meadow's face.

From its east end, a true fisherman's trail continues along the north bank, but by .1 mile it becomes too restricted to follow. A second trail fragment along the south bank parallels its course. When the water level permits a crossing, the hiker can trace the south bank for another .2 mile, then crisscross the creek utilizing angler and elk trails, stone crossings, and a minimum of wading to explore upstream. In explorations along the water, beware of nettles.

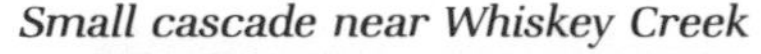

Small cascade near Whiskey Creek

28 SOUTH HILLS RIDGELINE TO SPENCER BUTTE LOOP

Distance: 6.6 miles round trip, but hike may be extended
Elevation Change: 1200 feet
Difficulty: Moderate
Maps: USGS Cottage Grove; South Hills Ridgeline Trail Map & Guide
Water: Carry water
Season: All year
For More Information: Eugene Parks, Recreation and Cultural Services

The South Hills Ridgeline Trail on the southern outskirts of Eugene successfully retains its wild character, affording an ideal retreat. The trail tours mature second-growth and old-growth stands, woodlands, and meadows, introducing the variety and texture of the hills. Only where the trail dips down to the roads for the five trailhead accesses do the sight and sound of civilization intrude.

The trail presents a rich botanical area; flowers bloom from March through August. Beneath a canopy of conifer, oak, maple, dogwood, and madrone, members of the heath, orchid, lily, and rose families sprinkle the hillside with color. The rare wayside aster adds its blooms in July.

The Spencer Butte area boasts the greatest variety of ferns

Dogwood

found anywhere in Oregon. Sword, bracken, lady, and wood fern find suitable habitat here.

From atop Spencer Butte (elevation 2062 feet), the hiker secures panoramic viewing of the cityscape of Eugene; the Cascades, featuring the Three Sisters and Mt. Jefferson; the Willamette Valley; and the foothills of the Coast Range. Often, when fog fills the valley, Spencer Butte basks in the sun, offering exciting views of a vast sea of clouds punctured by the Cascades to the east and the foothills to the west.

To reach the easternmost trailhead from Interstate 5, take the 30th Avenue Exit. Travel west on 30th Avenue 3.2 miles, and take a left onto Hilyard. In less than a quarter mile, take another left and drive 1.1 miles on East Amazon, then turn left onto Dillard Road. The trailhead lies 2 miles ahead on the right.

From the parking area, the trail traces Dillard Road north for 100 yards before it dips into the woods. Autumn welcomes the hiker to this woodland bounty with a colorful mat of bigleaf maple leaves. Side trails branching to the left rejoin the main trail at .2 mile.

Blackberry vines, sword and bracken fern, snowberry, and Oregon grape weave the understory, while lichen and mosses soften the outlines of the scattered stumps. Nearing the point where the trails merge, madrone enters the forest mix, along with some small oaks and alders. Insect galls riddle the underside of the oak leaves.

The trail advances with its easy, rolling nature to the Fox Hollow trailhead (.8 mile). From the stairs, a left leads to the parking area. The trail then turns right, traveling along Fox Hollow Road and crossing it in 50 yards.

Once back on the trail, a small bridge over a spring showcases an army of horsetail reeds. Their height and number invite the hiker to pause. At 1.2 miles, steps mount the slope. Where the trail branches, the left fork represents the main trail.

Soon thereafter, the hiker arrives at a sign-marked junction. Following the steps uphill to the left leads to the Spencer Butte Loop. Continuing straight ahead leads to the remainder of the South Hills Ridgeline Trail and an opportunity to extend this hike.

Opting for the loop, the hiker climbs into greater old-growth abundance. Sword ferns spill from the hillside, and a varied groundcover, thick with mosses, paints the forest floor green. A shortcut charges straight up the hill, but following the more graduated course of the trail prevents additional erosion.

In the meadow at 2 miles, the hiker arrives at the Spencer Butte Loop. Going left for a clockwise tour of the loop provides a good cardiovascular workout and a less taxing descent for the

Cloud-filled Willamette Valley from Spencer Butte

knees. The trail departs the meadow, descending through a second-growth forest dotted by a few old-timers and marked by sparse groundcover. At 2.2 miles, the trail advances along a boardwalk that can become treacherous when wet. Use of the rail is recommended. Leaving the boardwalk, the trail's descent moderates.

In a quarter mile, the trail passes the Spencer Butte Park picnic area. The loop continuation lies past the restrooms; it's the trail branch to the right, just above the stairs to the parking lot.

Without ceremony, this stretch of trail reveals its character—a no-nonsense .5-mile ascent to the summit of Spencer Butte. A wire fence in disrepair borders and defines the trail, which travels over the boulder and rock surface of the butte's west face. Wooden steps and metal rungs facilitate footing, but the trail is not difficult, just steep.

At 2.8 miles, the hiker gains an early view to the north and west. The trail then briefly pulls out onto a grassy slope. When it returns to the forest the hiker can either streak up the slope on the skyward stairs or pursue the more gradual summit approach of the trail.

The final ascent becomes confused, with the true trail hidden among the many imposters. It's anyone's guess. The summit features views of Eugene and the Willamette Valley, the Cascades and the Coast Range. A rocky outpost provides the vantage, while the wide back of the butte beckons with new perspectives on the panorama.

The loop continues with the trail descending from the butte's northwest end. On the west face, trail fragments riddle the first .1 mile, but quickly the true trail reveals itself, advancing generally southeast as it zigzags down the slope.

Leaving the open cap of the summit, the trail returns to old-growth forest and an earthen bed. When wet, the tree roots across the trail make for slippery footing. Caution is advised.

When the trail returns to the meadow at 4.6 miles, a left turn leads to a signed junction. Here, a right returns the hiker to the Dillard Road trailhead. A left extends the hike.

Venturing farther west along the Ridgeline Trail, the hiker encounters more of the old-growth environment. In late fall, mushrooms and galls ornament the leaf mat. In a short while, the trail crosses a bridge over a runoff, where alder and thimbleberry gain a stronghold. The trail then descends west by northwest reaching the trailhead on Willamette Road in 1.2 miles. An additional 1.5 miles of trail tour the hills west of Willamette Road, with the trail access just north of 52nd West.

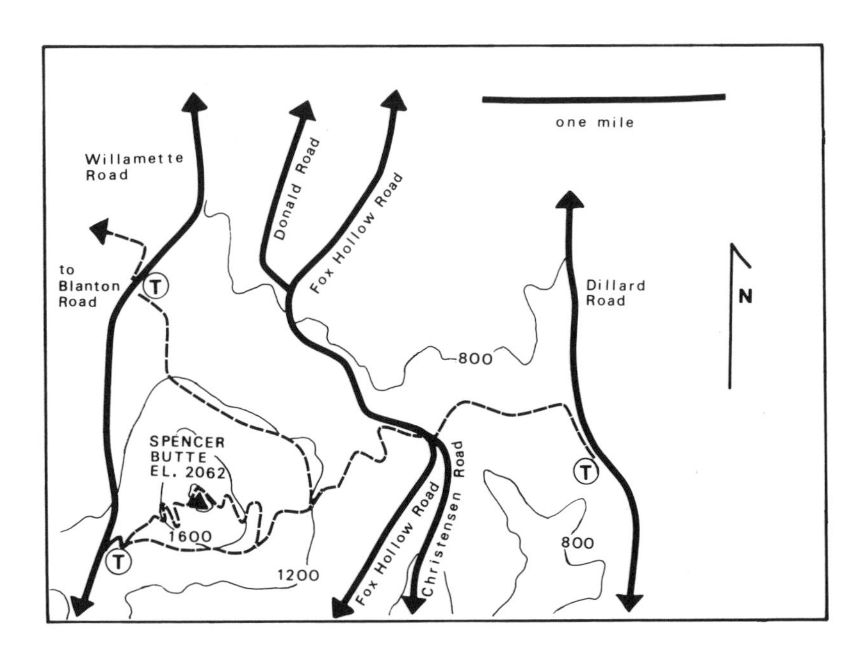

29 SILTCOOS LAKE

Distance: 4.1 miles round trip
Elevation Change: 300 feet
Difficulty: Easy
Map: Oregon Dunes National Recreation Area
Water: Siltcoos Lake
Season: All year
For More Information: Oregon Dunes National Recreation Area

The dark cloak of a Sitka spruce–Douglas fir second-growth coastal forest envelops this trail. Deprived of light and nutrients, the groundcover is strikingly sparse. The monotony of this single-story forest is overwhelming. Salal, sword and deer fern, and red and black huckleberry provide only patchy accents. Only the moist bottomlands along the spring-fed streams support giant ferns and rich moss coverings, common to the Coast Range.

In marked contrast to the forest sparsity is the varied habitat of Siltcoos Lake. Willow, alder, slough sedge, and salmonberry thrive along the marshy shore, with reeds and cattails guarding the water's edge. In the shallow waters, tangles of water lilies and mats of duckweed color the surface. Such lakeside diversity supports deer, rabbits, newts, salamanders, cormorants, and ducks, virtually guaranteeing a wildlife sighting.

With the trail conveniently located off U.S. 101, it's a nice complement to an Oregon coast vacation. To reach the trailhead from

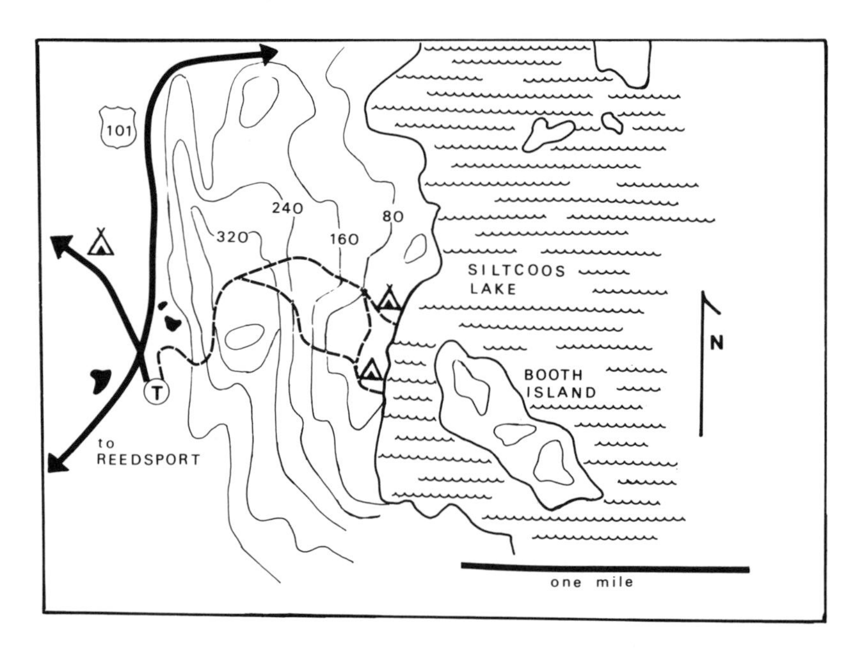

Old-growth stump beside Siltcoos Lake Trail

the junction of U.S. 101 and Oregon 38 north of Reedsport, hikers drive 13.3 miles north on U.S. 101. From the junction of U.S. 101 and Oregon 126 in Florence, they travel 7.7 miles south. The trailhead turnoff is on the highway's east side, near milepost 198, just opposite the Siltcoos Dunes/Beach Access of the Oregon Dunes National Recreation Area.

The trail first enters a disturbed environment of tree falls, brush, sword fern, and huckleberry—an area that surprisingly hosts some 66 bird species. Birders will want to come armed with identification guides and binoculars.

At .3 mile, the steps on the left mark the beginning of the trail proper. Here, a second-growth coastal forest replaces the disturbed environment. The trail is easy and winding, with gradual dips and rises.

At .7 mile, the trail splits to make a loop. The north route to the lake, built in 1987, journeys through a similar single-story Sitka spruce forest. The numerous stumps of the cedar monarchs from forests past capture the hiker's imagination. Winter rains and new growth have already softened the hard edges of the recent construction, blending the trail with its setting.

At 1.6 miles, the trail bypasses a campsite along the north end of the lake. Five secluded campsites dot this north section of shoreline, with a secondary trail sewing them together. In another 10 yards, the trail meets with the southern route of the loop.

A right turn at the junction begins the return to U.S. 101. The trail meanders inland through forest and travels via a boardwalk over a spring-fed stream and marshy bottomland to reach the south camp junction in .5 mile. From here, one can again see the lake through the trees. Taking a left delivers a single campsite on the Siltcoos shore, in a quarter mile. Cormorants and herons frequently perch on the lake-isolated snags, as salamanders ripple the shallow waters near shore. Rusting iron remnants from logging days lie on the bank.

The campsites along the lake are complete with tables and grills and nearby vault toilets. The ease of this trail and its pleasant destination recommend it to the backpacking newcomer.

When ready to venture on, backtrack to the main loop and take a left to continue the southern tour of the forest. In winter, downfalls toppled by wind gusts litter the trail section that lies below the neighboring clearcut. Maintenance crews generally clear away these obstacles prior to the peak hiking season.

30 KENTUCKY FALLS

Distance: 4 miles round trip
Elevation Change: 1000 feet
Difficulty: Moderate
Maps: USGS Goodwin Peak; USFS Siuslaw National Forest
Water: Kentucky Creek and North Fork Smith River
Season: All year (in winter, call regarding road conditions)
For More Information: Mapleton Ranger District

This trail wanders through beautiful old-growth forest and second-growth Douglas fir to deliver the hiker to a waterfall spectacular. Three waterfalls approximately 80 to 90 feet high dazzle the visitor. Their thunder resounds in the canyons. With the winter rains, thick veils of chilling mist peel off the falls and catch the wind, painting the forest setting with mystery.

But, it is the old-growth setting that makes the trail such a pleasurable discovery. Red and evergreen huckleberry, deer and sword fern, and jagged-topped snags engage the eye and soothe the spirit. Deer and elk, woodpeckers and varied thrushes deliver the surprise attractions of the trail.

Currently, the trail concludes at the two lower falls, but the Forest Service has flagged an additional 5 miles of trail following the North Fork Smith River downstream. While the recent Forest

Douglas fir bridges the banks of Kentucky Creek.

Plan draft calls for the area of the three falls to be designated a special-interest area, the North Fork Smith River below the falls would be excluded from the protective designation.

Touring this trail requires a drive. North of Reedsport, the route heads east on County 48 and 48A before exiting north onto Forest SR 23. A left from Forest SR 23 onto 2300.919 goes 2.7 miles to the Kentucky Falls trailhead on the left. Parking, for up to five cars, is on the right.

An alternate approach from Oregon 126 begins 8.8 miles east of the Archie Knowles Campground or 6 miles west of the Walton Store and Post Office. Turn south toward the Whittaker Creek Recreation Area. Go 1.5 miles and take a right turn. In another 1.5 miles, bear left onto Dunn Ridge Road. After another 6.9 miles, take a left on the gravel road to Reedsport. In 2.7 miles, take a right onto Forest SR 23 for 1.6 miles, then take a right onto 2300.919 to reach the Kentucky Falls trailhead in 2.7 miles. Major junctions en route to the trail are well marked.

The beginning portion of trail parallels Kentucky Creek and plunges the hiker into old-growth abundance. Alder and salmonberry push creekside, while salal, deer and sword fern, and Oregon grape flood the understory. The trail assumes a fairly even course the first half mile.

Soon, the hiker arrives at an overlook of Upper Kentucky Falls. From here, the trail zigzags down the rocky cliff to the base of the

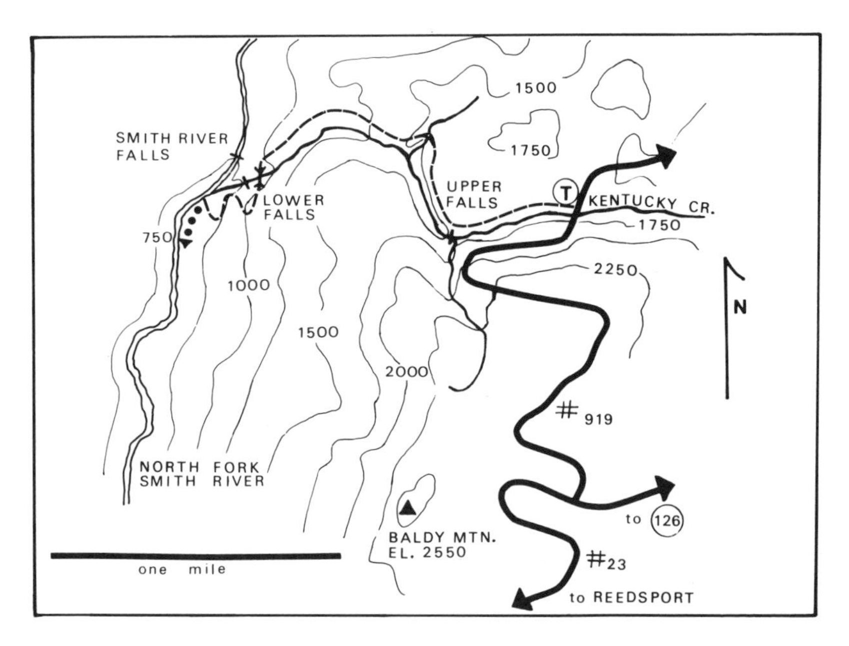

falls (.75 mile). The upper falls alone would justify the trail's existence.

Situated in a beautiful canyon, Upper Kentucky Falls is a study of power in winter and grace in summer. Stalwart rock islands disrupt the water's downward course, lending character to the falls. Watery jewels ornament the nearby plants pushing through the rock crevices.

At the upcoming bridge over a side creek, the trail briefly pulls away from Kentucky Creek. Rhododendron showers the snagtops, adding color and charm to the old-growth forest. At 1.4 miles, the trail crosses Kentucky Creek on the back of a tree bridge. At 1.6 miles, the creek drops rapidly away from the trail.

For the next .4 mile, the trail switchbacks down to the level of the creek and the North Fork Smith River. Here, one obtains the vantage on Lower Kentucky Falls and Smith River Falls. The simultaneous presence of the two falls amplifies the beauty and excitement of the setting, without stealing from the glory of either one.

Winter offers the best viewing, for then the falls roar with water and the maples lose their leaves, opening up the vista. Moss-covered boulders and logs litter the base of the falls. In the summer of 1988, the Forest Service constructed a viewing deck, allowing easy access to viewpoints and photo points.

The falls command a lengthy appreciation. When ready, return the way you came.

31 GOLDEN AND SILVER FALLS

Distance: 3.3 miles round trip (total distance for three trails)
Elevation Change: 300 feet
Difficulty: Easy
Map: USGS Ivers Peak
Water: Glenn Creek and Silver Creek
Season: All year
For More Information: District State Parks Headquarters, Sunset Bay State Park

Golden and Silver Falls State Park features two spectacular 200-foot waterfalls and the scenic creekbeds of Glenn and Silver creeks. Three trail segments introduce the hiker to the area. A fourth at one time promised a good view of Silver Falls, but its vista point is now overgrown.

Bigleaf maple, alder, and fern accent the beauty of the creeks. Myrtle, blackberry, and rhododendron complement the old-growth forest. Sandstone cliffs occasionally define the course of the trails and prescribe the waterfalls themselves.

Weyerhaeuser dedicated Silver Falls and its surrounding area to the people of Oregon on April 14, 1935. In 1936 the extraordinary beauty of the stand of Douglas firs, showcasing the two falls and cloaking the creek canyons, spurred the State Park System to

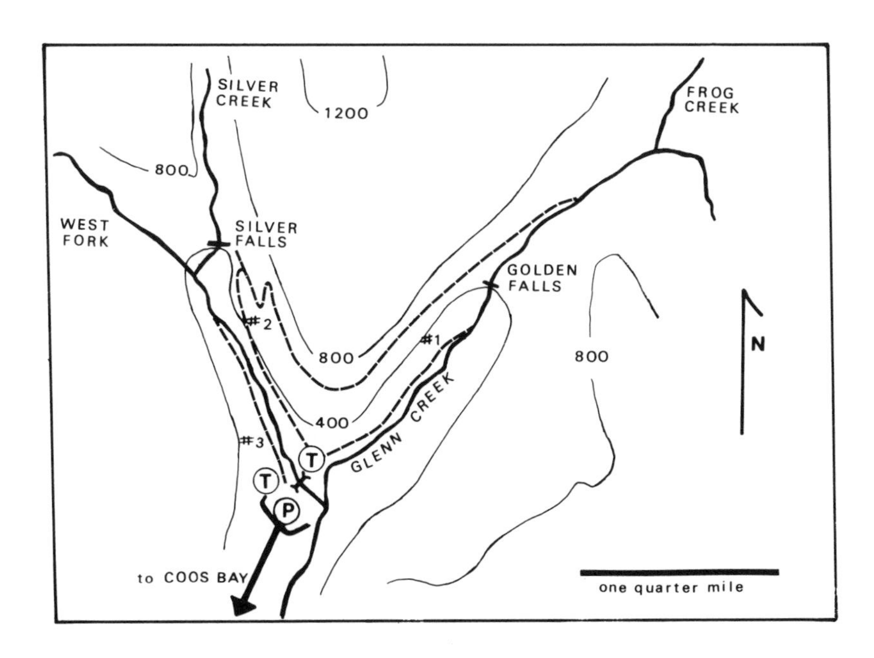

seek preservation of the remainder of the area, beginning with the land of the Waterford Lumber Company near Golden Falls. Today the park measures some 157 acres.

To reach the state park from Coos Bay, exit east off U.S. 101 at the sign reading "to Allegany." In 1.1 miles, at the intersection of D and 6th in Coos Bay, take a right on D Street. Follow the signs to Golden and Silver Falls State Park. The park lies approximately 24 miles northeast of Coos Bay. There are picnic tables and vault toilets for visitor convenience.

Trail segment #1 branches to the right as one enters the picnic area from the Silver Creek bridge. It traces the north bank of Glenn Creek, leading to the base of Golden Falls in a quarter mile. This is an impressive thundering falls, particularly following the winter rains. The water races down the sandstone face before spreading in cascades over the boulder-littered base. Watery jewels accent the mosses and oxalis trailside. Return as you came.

Trail segment #2 branches to the left, following the Silver Creek crossing. This trail assumes an elevated course along the hill behind the picnic area. Overlooks of Silver Creek and its lush green canyon accent the first portion of this trail.

At .3 mile, a 50-foot spur departs to the left, leading to the Silver Falls viewpoint. From here, the hiker gains a side view of the falls. In its full booming glory, Silver Falls kicks up a soaking spray, discouraging a lengthy appraisal. In the dry season, this viewpoint promises a calmer vantage on a ribbony falls.

As it leaves the viewpoint, the trail continues switchbacking up the hill, then winds around the sandstone outcrop to arrive at the top of Golden Falls and a viewpoint (.75 mile).

The trail then continues upstream, paralleling Glenn Creek. Old-growth plant life crowds both sides of the trail. At 1 mile, the trail intersects an old, abandoned road. Going to the right, the trail ends at Glenn Creek in about .1 mile. The opposite direction leads to a clearcut. Return the way you came.

The third trail segment offers a drier perspective on Silver Falls. This trail starts from the left-hand side of the parking area. It follows Silver Creek upstream, and it ends at the viewpoint in .3 mile. From here, Silver Falls takes on the appearance of flowstone, exhibiting not only power but also beauty. A bench invites a lingering study. A bronze plaque denotes the original Weyerhaeuser gift of this land to Coos County in 1935. Again, return as you came.

Golden Falls, Golden and Silver Falls State Park

32 ELK CREEK FALLS

Distance: 2.7 miles round trip
Elevation Change: 700 feet
Difficulty: Moderate
Maps: USGS Powers; USFS Siskiyou National Forest
Water: Elk Creek
Season: All year
For More Information: Powers Ranger District

Elk Creek Falls and the world's largest Port Orford cedar mark the limits of this trail. Introducing the trail, Elk Creek Falls presents the unified charm and beauty of a pulsing veil of water, delicate greenery, and a black cliff face. Closing the trail, the champion cedar stands 219 feet high and has a circumference of nearly 38 feet. It is the centerpiece to a grove of giant firs and cedars.

The trail itself climbs through beautiful old-growth forest. Accenting its course are bigleaf maple, myrtle, and rhododendron, with rushes of sword, deer, and maidenhair ferns. The fallen trees along the way make interesting studies with the great gouges they leave in their wakes. The old growth provides a dramatic contrast to the neighboring reforested clearcut.

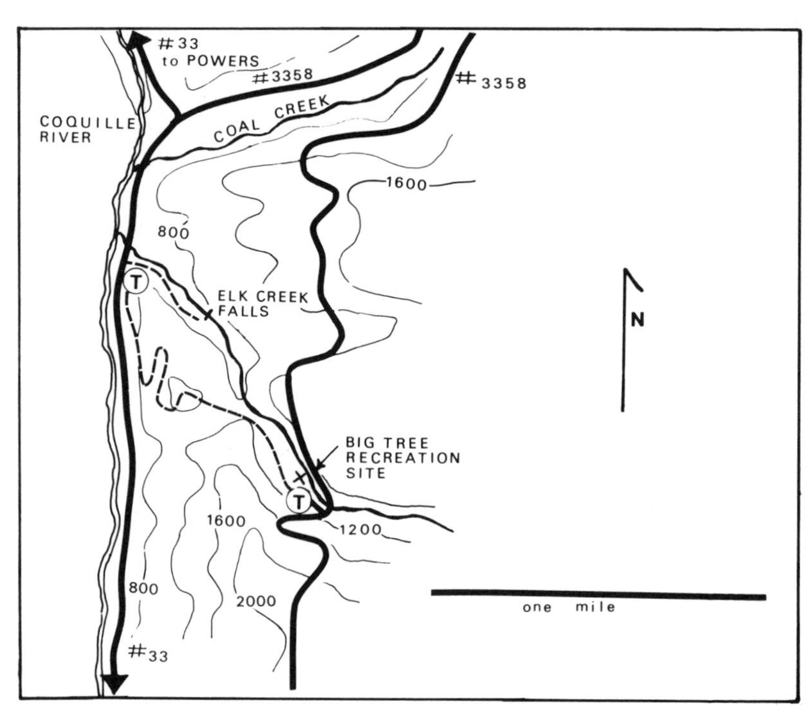

Elk Creek Falls

At the Big Tree Recreation Site, home of the champion Port Orford cedar, several tree and plant species are identified with plaques.

To reach the trail from Powers, travel south 6.1 miles on County 219, which later becomes Forest SR 33. The turnouts for trailhead parking are on the east side of Forest SR 33. The trailhead is marked.

From the trailhead marker, the fork to the left leads to Elk Creek Falls and the picnic area in .1 mile. Elk Creek Falls is a ribbony, two-segment falls adorned by the moss it nourishes. Its gentle beauty captivates onlookers. For closer viewing, the sure-footed can hopscotch up the rocky creekbed to the base of the falls.

The trail uphill to the right leads to the record-setting Port Orford cedar and the Big Tree Recreation Site. The trail begins with a steady and relatively steep uphill charge for the first half mile. With the gain in elevation, more light penetrates and the myrtle and rhododendron thrive. From here, the trail traces the ridgetop. A recovering clearcut occupies the view to the left.

At .7 mile, the trail draws deeper into the old growth and away from the clearcut, then undulates before delivering the hiker to a forest road at 1 mile. From here, take a right and walk up the road about 30 yards. The trail resumes on the opposite side, cutting through a grassy patch. Where the trail re-enters the trees, there's a sign pointing back toward Elk Creek Falls.

The trail now tours an area rich with bigleaf maple, hemlock, and fern, before exiting onto the road to the Big Tree Recreation Site. A left on the road leads to the stairs over the fallen Douglas fir. The viewing stage for the champion cedar lies to the left at 1.25 miles.

Neighboring large cedars and firs create a shady retreat, as the tree-identification signs beg to be read and the grove explored. The grove's picnic sites number among Oregon's most scenic, extending an invitation that's difficult to refuse.

Return as you came.

33 JOHNSON AND SUCKER CREEKS

Distance: 5 miles round trip
Elevation Change: 800 feet
Difficulty: Moderate
Maps: USGS Powers and Agness; USFS Siskiyou National Forest
Water: Johnson and Sucker creeks
Season: All year
For More Information: Powers Ranger District

This trail tours a variety of environments, beginning with the quiet beauty of Sucker Creek. Such scenic creeks and rivers are a trademark of the coastal mountain corridor. Red alder and bigleaf maple overhang Sucker Creek's rippling, clear water, while rocky bars and an occasional downfall alter its course.

Sucker Creek

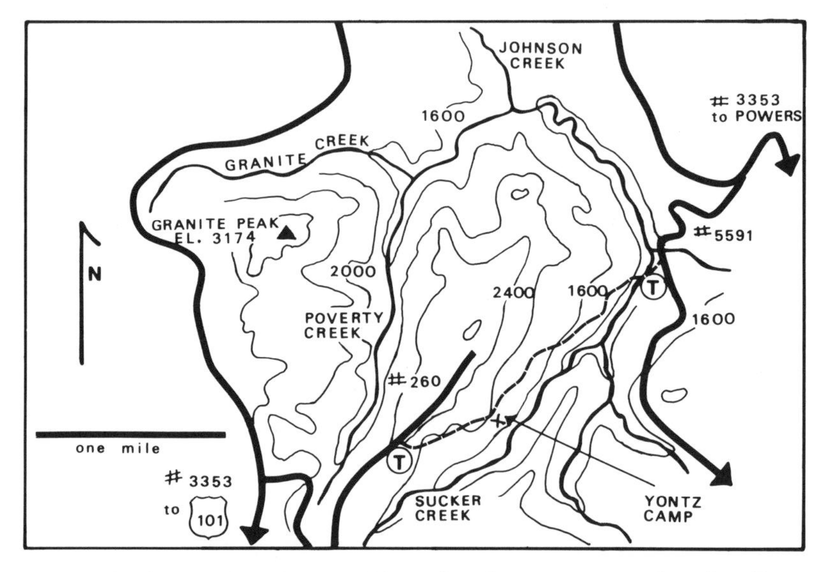

A lush old-growth forest of Douglas fir, western red cedar, Port Orford cedar, western hemlock, and a treasury of mosses and groundcover next claim the trail, only to deliver it to the drier slopes of madrone, canyon live oak, and tanoak. Rhododendron laces much of the forest complex, promising a springtime spectacle. But, it is the solitude and the forest tranquility that recommend this trail.

Entering from Powers, travel south 10.8 miles on County 219, which later becomes Forest SR 33. Turn right onto Forest SR 3353 and continue 3.1 miles to the junction with Forest SR 5591. Turn left onto Forest SR 5591. The trailhead is to the right in 1.4 miles, just beyond the Johnson Creek bridge. A second trailhead off Forest SR 3353.260 lies approximately 12 miles west of the Forest SR 33-Forest SR 3353 junction.

Entering from U.S. 101, take Elk River Road east and follow the signs to Powers, exiting onto Forest SR 3353.260 or Forest SR 5591 for the trailheads.

Beginning from the trailhead near the Johnson Creek bridge on Forest SR 5591, the trail exits the far end of the turnout and follows the east bank of Sucker Creek for about 200 yards. On the opposite shore, ribbons mark where the trail continues.

It's a fairly easy, wet crossing, or there is a cable-secured log that one can shimmy across to avoid cold, wet feet in the springtime. (The log's width discourages an upright crossing.) Later in the hiking season, a stone-hop crossing is possible.

Once on the opposite side, the hiker enters a beautiful old-growth gallery: cool, shaded, and brimming with greenery. The trail quickly climbs above Sucker Creek on a steady upward grade. At one-half mile, the trail briefly tours an area touched by fire. Charred trunks and spare groundcover record its passage. In another .2 mile, the canyon pinches together at a dry creek crossing.

At this point, the hiker should take a moment to note the location and appearance of the trail just walked. A good unmaintained trail departs uphill from this point, just above the established trail. This second trail can mislead the hiker on the return trip.

Cascades of fern shower the trail's shoulder, as it draws deeper into the forest and away from Sucker Creek Canyon. At 2 miles, the hiker arrives at the spur to Yontz Camp. The camp lies 100 yards downslope. It is not much more than a clearing with some well-placed logs, but the area boasts some stout old-growth firs, towering cedars, and a bounty of rhododendron.

Leaving the camp, the trail soon enters a much drier environment of madrone, tanoak, and canyon live oak. The trail becomes rocky and passes over a couple of small slide areas. There are a few showings of poison oak along this final leg, as well as showings of succulent varieties and alp-lily.

There is little shade from here to the trail's close at the parking area off Forest SR 3353.260. Hikers return the way they came.

Fording Sucker Creek

34 BARKLOW MOUNTAIN

Distance: 2 miles round trip (can be easily extended with unmaintained trail)
Elevation Change: 300 feet
Difficulty: Easy
Maps: USGS Powers and Agness; USFS Siskiyou National Forest
Water: Unnamed creek below Barklow Camp
Season: Spring through fall
For More Information: Powers Ranger District

Barklow Mountain (elevation 3579 feet) was named for a well-known pioneer family of Coos County. The site of a former lookout, its tower was razed in the 1970s. The advent of satellites ended the lookout's usefulness, and the aging tower proved a liability.

Despite the tower's absence, the mostly open top of Barklow Mountain continues to provide exceptional views. The Coast Range, the ocean, the Grassy Knob Wilderness, Copper and Salmon mountains, and the faint outline of the distant Cascades comprise the panorama. Barklow Mountain also has easy access, welcoming hikers of all capabilities.

Barklow Camp was at one time a wayside for the trail crews and linesmen working on the lookout communication lines. The site itself is a former meadow.

The mountain hosts a transition-zone climate, with Douglas fir and Oregon grape mixing with manzanita and tanoak. Salal, rhododendron, knobcone pine, and live oak complete the vegetation mix.

To reach the trailhead from U.S. 101, turn east on Elk River Road, north of Port Orford. In 7.5 miles, near the fish hatchery, the road officially becomes Forest SR 5325. Pavement ends in 5.3 miles, and the route continues along the dirt road 5.6 miles to the junction with Forest SR 5201. Take a right to follow Forest SR 5325 toward Powers. At the road junction in 8.8 miles, take a left turn onto Forest SR 3353 for 9.6 miles. From here, a left turn uphill on Forest SR 220 leads to the trailhead in 1.3 miles.

Entering from Powers, take County 219/Forest SR 33 south for 10.8 miles, turning right onto Forest SR 3353. After traveling another 10.7 miles, a right uphill on Forest SR 220 leads to the trailhead.

From the trailhead, the easy-winding trail climbs through Douglas fir, rhododendron, and manzanita to the trail junction at .4 mile. The trail uphill to the right leads to the former lookout site and a rewarding overlook of the Coast Range and Grassy

Barklow Camp

Knob Wilderness in .1 mile. The shortness and ease of the trail to Barklow Mountain suggest a lingering stay, with perhaps a picnic lunch or sunset vigil.

Taking the left fork leads to Barklow Camp, in an additional half mile. The trail section to the camp has only recently been reopened. It slices the manzanita-cloaked south slope of Barklow Mountain, before descending into a second-growth forest of Douglas fir, western red cedar, salal, and Oregon grape. The standing structure of the old hut, tin cans, broken glass, and a rusted wood stove signal the arrival at the camp. Do not disturb the property, and watch out for nails.

In the salal flat above the hut, the hiker will detect the faint outline of the original trail that continues rounding Barklow Mountain. Once through the patch, this unmaintained trail again

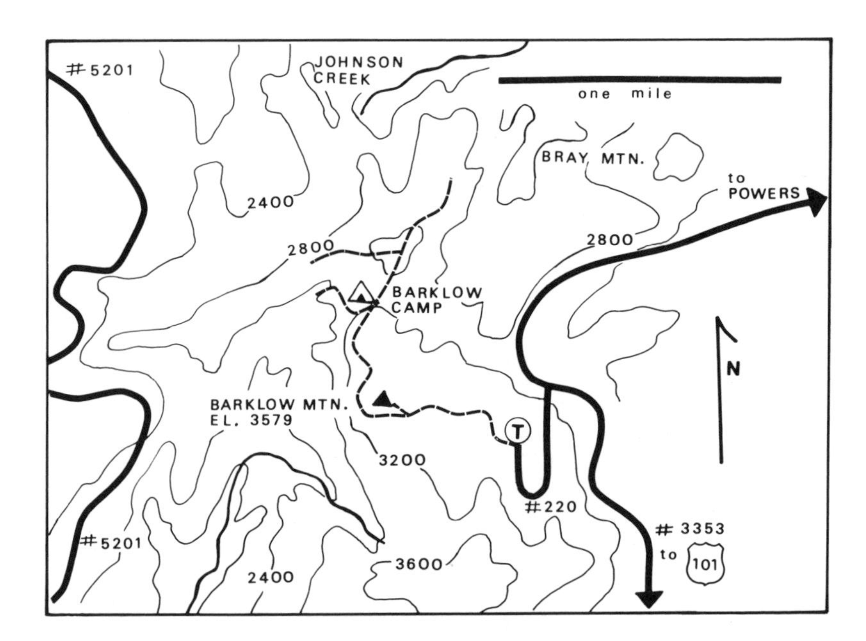

clears and is easy to follow. In a quarter mile, it meets the old Johnson Creek Trail, shown on the topo.

Straight ahead, the trail continues in fairly good condition for another .5 mile. The major obstacle is the scattered patches of thick salal. The trail halts on a saddle in a former clearcut, now probably 20 years into its recovery. Thick manzanita, small fir, rhododendron, tanoak, and chinquapin dress the slope. The saddle features views of Bray Mountain, Granite Peak, the Johnson Creek drainage, and points east.

The trail segment that heads left at the Johnson Creek Trail junction is currently being considered by the Forest Service for reopening. When completed the proposed trail will meet Forest SR 5201, emerge, and continue on to Elk River.

Meanwhile, the trail takes a couple of switchbacks downhill, then continues along a ridge. Salal riddles the trail. Later, in the recovering clearcut, manzanita, tanoak, and canyon live oak encroach on the path. While the trail remains discernible, the density of the brush discourages all but the hardy after about .3 mile.

The unmaintained trail leading downhill from the hut is the trail to the camp's water source—an unnamed creek no more than a quarter mile from the camp.

Despite their unmaintained status, these trails welcome short investigations. Any one would make a nice extension to the trek.

Return the way you came.

35 COQUILLE RIVER FALLS

Distance: 1.1 miles round trip
Elevation Change: 600 feet
Difficulty: Easy
Maps: USGS Agness; USFS Siskiyou National Forest
Water: South Fork Coquille River
Season: All year
For More Information: Powers Ranger District

The star feature of this trail is Coquille River Falls, with its upper triple set of falls feeding the lower double set, all arranged in a moss-mantled rock bowl. This downward rush of water is a spectacle of power and beauty, swollen by the rains of winter.

Housing this spectacle is the Coquille River Falls Natural Area, which showcases a beautiful old-growth forest of cedar, hemlock, myrtle, and Douglas fir. The understory bursts with Oregon grape, oxalis, blackberry, and red and black huckleberry. Near the river, alder and bigleaf maple reign above a fern-covered floor.

Lower Coquille River Falls, late summer

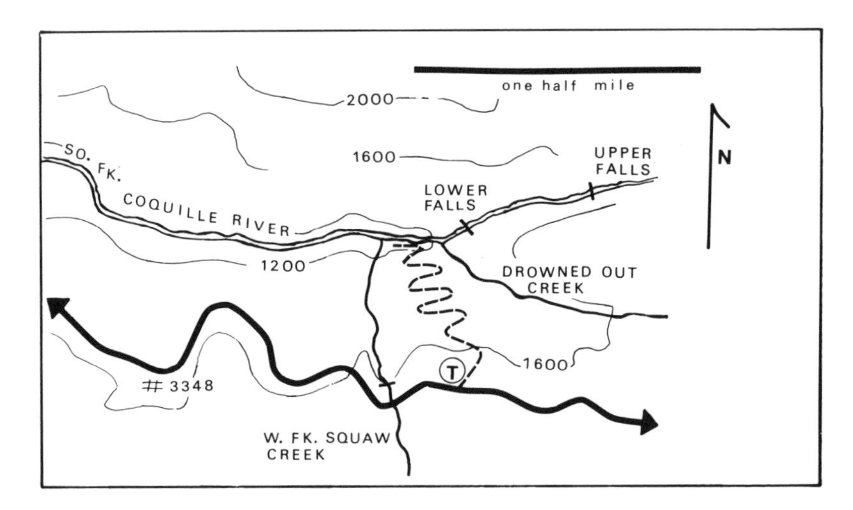

During the dry season, a rock scramble to the upper falls is possible. A plaque dedicated to the memory of a local scout who fell near the lower falls reminds the cross-country hiker that the rocks command respect. With rains and high waters, the trail alone leads the discovery.

From Powers, travel south 16.5 miles on County 219, which later becomes Forest SR 33. A left turn onto Forest SR 3348 leads to the trailhead on the left in 1.5 miles, just beyond the Squaw Creek bridge.

Without ceremony, a quick succession of switchbacks delivers the hiker to the Coquille River Falls viewpoint (.5 mile). The plunge downhill discourages a lengthy study of the rich forest habitat that secludes the trail. This appreciation is best reserved for the return trek uphill.

The final approach to the falls viewpoint requires caution. The leaf mat, often damp with spray, provides treacherous footing, particularly once Coquille River Falls captures the hiker's attention.

When temperatures drop, the spray freezes, compounding the difficulty of the descent, but transforming the setting. Icicles drip from the tips of sword ferns, and a frost mosaic tops each blackberry leaf.

A second falls viewpoint lies 100 yards farther down the trail. This post offers views of both the upper and lower sets of falls. Again, caution in the descent is advised.

In a dry year, the hiker can reach the base of the upper falls with an easy rock scramble. The best place to stage an ascent is from the spur that leaves the trail just above the first viewpoint and crosses Drowned Out Creek.

Above Lower Coquille River Falls, the cross-country hiker finds quiet emerald pools dotting the course. Boulder jumbles and weathered logs accent the waters. Naturally scoured mortars, some several inches deep, pockmark the exposed rock. Ahead, Upper Coquille River Falls thunders, and a thrilling overview of Coquille River Canyon awaits.

36 PANTHER RIDGE

Distance: 11.2 miles one way, including Hanging Rock spur (accessed by five trailheads, this trail welcomes shorter day hikes)
Elevation Change: 1500 feet
Difficulty: Strenuous
Maps: USGS Agness, Marial, and Bone Mountain; USFS Siskiyou National Forest or Kalmiopsis Wilderness/Wild Rogue Wilderness
Water: Carry water
Season: Spring through fall
For More Information: Powers Ranger District

This trail ties together Buck Point and the Bald Knob Lookout on Panther Ridge, tracing part of the Rogue River Valley skyline. Nearly 75 percent of the trail falls in the Wild Rogue Wilderness, a buffer for the Wild and Scenic River.

The woodland setting of the trail is a treasure-trove of old growth and diverse vegetation. Cedars, Douglas fir, knobcone pine, tanoak, manzanita, and chinquapin generate a forest of texture and surprise. Deer dart between the boundary clearcut and the shelter of the forest.

But Hanging Rock is the outstanding feature of this trail, both literally and figuratively. This ridgeline outcrop protrudes over the Rogue Valley, affording unrivaled views of it, neighboring Eden Valley, and the forest beyond. In dizzying display, violet-green swallows dip and dart from crannies below the dome summit.

In the future, the hiker may be able to explore the Clay Hill Trail, which joins Panther Ridge to the Rogue River Valley. The Forest Service is presently evaluating the possibility of this trail's reopening.

To reach Panther Ridge, travel south from Powers on County 219, which later becomes Forest SR 33. In 16.5 miles, the route turns east onto Forest SR 3348. On the right, in 2 miles, is the turnoff for Forest SR 5520 and the Bald Knob Lookout. This turn leads to the westernmost trailheads.

A rich understory of rhododendron characterizes the Panther Ridge Trail.

To reach the Buck Point trailhead (the beginning point for this trail description), continue on Forest SR 3348 another 7 miles, turning south onto Forest SR 5520 near Buck Creek. After 1.2 miles, a turn left onto Forest SR 5520.230 leads to the trailhead in .7 mile.

The trail to Buck Point begins with a steady climb through open forest, despite the bounty of rhododendron, salal, ferns, and moss-draped firs. Hot summer days require extra water.

The Panther Ridge Trail boasts the finest showcase of rhododendron in the coastal mountains. Late spring to early summer marks the favorite time to tour the trail.

As the trail mounts the ridge, vanilla leaf, candy-stick, and lupine take turns adding color and variety to the forest floor. At 1.5 miles, the hiker arrives at the junction for Hanging Rock. An open manzanita shrubland and nearby cliffs usher the hiker to Southern Oregon's geologic prize.

The area promises spectacular viewing, and Hanging Rock delivers it in .25 mile. Before the hiker lies the Rogue River Valley: Marial, the Mule Creek drainage, Paradise Bar, and Blossom Bar. Mt. Bolivar, Diamond Peak, and Saddle Peaks populate the skyline.

The outpost itself is a spectacle with its vertical walls and its prominence on the ridge. A lingering visit makes binoculars and camera worth their weight. (If time is limited, a shorter hike to Hanging Rock begins from the trailhead off Forest SR 5520.140).

To continue on the Panther Ridge Trail, hikers return to the junction and head west toward Clay Hill and Bald Knob. In .5 mile, the trail splits, with the branch to the right leading to the trailhead off Forest SR 5520.140. Straight ahead lies the continuation of the Panther Ridge tour.

The main trail soon becomes confused. Several paths streak the grassy slope ahead of the hiker. The true trail is that which follows the lowest course down the slope.

At 4.5 miles (measurement includes the Hanging Rock distance), the trail skirts a recovering clearcut. In another half mile, the hiker comes to the Panther Camp Trail junction. In .3 mile, this side trail arrives at a beautiful campsite above a long meadow. Groves of rhododendron crowd the meadow edge.

Staying on the Panther Ridge Trail, the hiker tours the slope above a recent clearcut before journeying through a corridor of young fir to the gravel pad at 6.3 miles. Here, the trail segments are unmarked. Note the way you came to avoid confusion on the return trip.

The trail leading to Bald Knob enters a group of trees to the southwest. A faded pink ribbon may mark the way. The trail now traces an overgrown road, meeting another road at 6.7 miles. Take a left turn for .2 mile to return to the forested path.

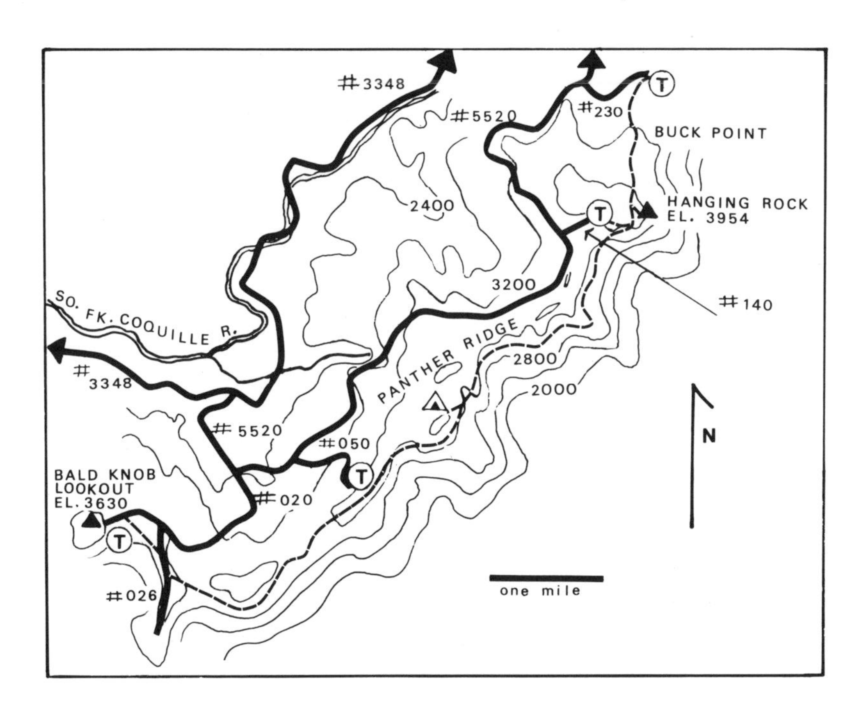

At 7.2 miles, the trail spur from Forest SR 5520.050 meets the Panther Ridge Trail. Late spring and early summer find the manzanita and knobcone pine of this stretch accented not only by rhododendron, but wild pea, dwarf star tulip, Indian paintbrush, and Columbia lily.

The trail segment that follows holds some steep downhill stretches. At 8.7 miles, clearcut and wilderness boundary face off at the trail. Hemlock and cedar abound both before and after the cut. The trail then undulates, finally climbing to Forest SR 5520.026 at 10 miles.

From this point, the trail turns right and follows the forest road for .25 mile. Find a sign inset from the road on the left to continue on the trail. The trail now follows a pretty, forested path, cool, dark, and rich with rhododendron. At 10.9 miles, the trail empties onto Forest SR 5520.020. Take a left turn to enjoy a .3-mile walk along the road to the Bald Knob Lookout Tower.

Bald Knob offers expansive views of the Rogue Valley, Big Bend, Mt. Bolivar, and the Wild Rogue Wilderness. The lookout attendant reports early morning sightings of elk, deer, and bear near the tower. The tower may be mounted at your own risk in numbers recommended by the posted sign.

37 MT. BOLIVAR

Distance: 3 miles round trip
Elevation Change: 1200 feet
Difficulty: Moderate
Maps: USGS Bone Mountain; USFS Siskiyou National Forest or Kalmiopsis Wilderness/Wild Rogue Wilderness
Water: Carry water
Season: Spring through fall
For More Information: Powers Ranger District

Mt. Bolivar (elevation 4319 feet) is the star feature of this orphaned corner of the Wild Rogue Wilderness. The trail climbs the mountain's steep, rugged flank in switchback fashion. The rocky terrain supports a pine–fir forest intermingled with manzanita, madrone, and chinquapin. An understory of rhododendron, bear grass, and lupine dashes the setting with color and variety.

The mountain received its name in 1900 from Coos County surveyor Simon Bolivar Cathcart. The name, though also his own, was intended as a tribute to the great Venezuelan liberator of that name. Since September 22, 1984, a commemorative plaque

View from summit, Mt. Bolivar

donated by the government of Venezuela has reflected the Oregon sun from atop Mt. Bolivar.

The summit offers 360-degree panoramic viewing of Eden Valley, the Rogue River Valley, Panther Ridge, and the Coquille River and Cow Creek drainages.

To reach Mt. Bolivar from Powers, go 16.5 miles south on County 219, which later becomes Forest SR 33. Turn east onto Forest SR 3348. After 18.1 miles, the road leaves Siskiyou Na-

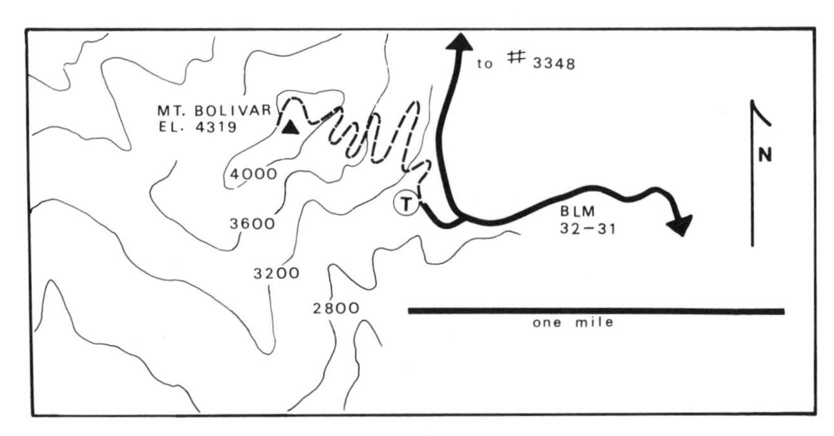

tional Forest and becomes BLM 32-31. In another 1.1 miles, a right turn leads to the Mt. Bolivar trailhead. Parking is uphill in .1 mile, or to the side of the road at the turn for low-clearance vehicles.

The trail begins its uphill course snaking through the mixed pine forest. Oregon grape, salal, fern, and vanilla leaf create an undergrowth tangle. Twin flowers and Columbia lily defy the rocky terrain, sprinkling delicacy and color along the trail.

The first stretch of trail is partially shaded and offers a steady, comfortable assault on the mountain. Flickers and chickadees flash their feathers, darting between branch and bush.

Early morning hikers may find their target under a halo of fog, but the valley clouds slowly rise once touched by the morning sun.

Nearing the halfway point, manzanita and chinquapin gain a stronghold, with the pines and firs becoming more scattered. Early vistas pique hiker anticipation of summit offerings.

At 1 mile, the trail circles around to the north side of Mt. Bolivar, where fir and hemlock shade its course. Rhododendron displays pom-pom finery, and fountains of fern color the forest floor.

From 1.2 miles to 1.5 miles, the character of the trail changes, with short, steep attacks on the summit. The final leg of the trail is exposed and hot. But the vista rewards the expended effort. Carry plenty of water.

Views of Diamond Peak, Saddle Peaks, Hanging Rock, the Wild Rogue Wilderness, Eden Valley, and the Coquille River drainage invite lengthy appreciation, while the monument from the Venezuelan government silently recalls history. A generous breeze sweeping the summit can be as stimulating as the view, and a valued companion on hot summer days.

Return as you came.

Rafting the Upper Rogue

38 UPPER ROGUE RIVER

Distance: 47 miles one way
Elevation Change: 700 feet
Difficulty: Strenuous
Maps: USGS Galice, Marial, and Agness; USFS Kalmiopsis Wilderness/Wild Rogue Wilderness or Siskiyou National Forest
Water: Rogue and its tributaries (*Giardia* present; purification required)
Season: All year
For More Information: Gold Beach Ranger District or the BLM office in Medford

This 47-mile National Recreation Trail journeys alongside 40 miles of beautiful, churning Rogue River, offering intimate views from sandy bars and riveting vistas from steep canyon walls. Narrow gorges, yawning passages, and white-water riffles shape the river's personality. Throughout the journey, the frequent changes in vegetation mix stimulate hiker interest.

The valley's history is also revealed along the way. The National Recreation Trail actually traces a one-time mining trail, meandering past the abandoned dreams of gold strikes, cabins, and farms. Whiskey Cabin and Rogue River Ranch, sidelights of the trail, are both on the National Register of Historic Places.

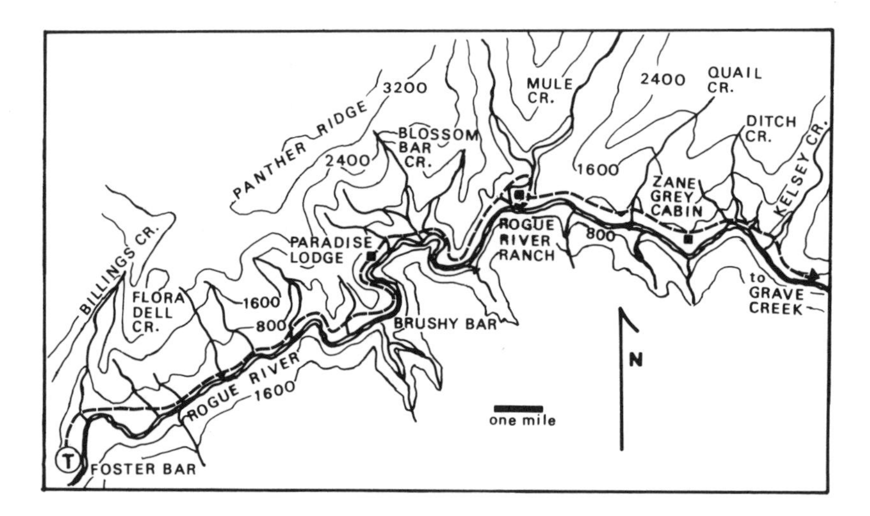

The National Forest Service has put together a guide to the Rogue River Trail, which is an excellent source to the area history. Important dates, events, and sites are noted. The drawback to this guide for the hiker is that, contrary to its name, it is written from the river traveler's perspective.

While the scenery and history of the Rogue River recommend this trail, the variety in wildlife sightings ranks among the best in the country. Black bear, river otter, mink, black- and white-tailed deer, ring-tailed cat, osprey, heron, and kingfisher add to an already unforgettable journey.

Grave Creek is the gateway to this prized overland excursion. From Interstate 5, take the Merlin exit, north of Grants Pass. Leaving the exit ramp, head north .2 mile, through a small business district, to turn left at Merlin–Galice Road. After 22 miles on Merlin–Galice Road and a crossing of the Grave Creek bridge, take a left to the boat ramp and trailhead.

There is no overnight parking in the boat-ramp lot. Along Merlin–Galice Road, however, there are several river tour/shuttle services, where one can arrange for a car pickup and shuttle to the closing trailhead. This service, although designed for rafters, is ideal for hikers, opening the entire 47 miles of trail for one-way exploration, without requiring a second vehicle.

The Upper Rogue Trail begins with a steep climb up the canyon wall of the north bank. Across the river, a second trail travels to Rainie Falls.

To date, the river rafting permit system appears a success. The hiker experiences a clean, unspoiled Rogue River Valley with ample opportunity for solitude and reflection, while rafters continue to sample the river thrills.

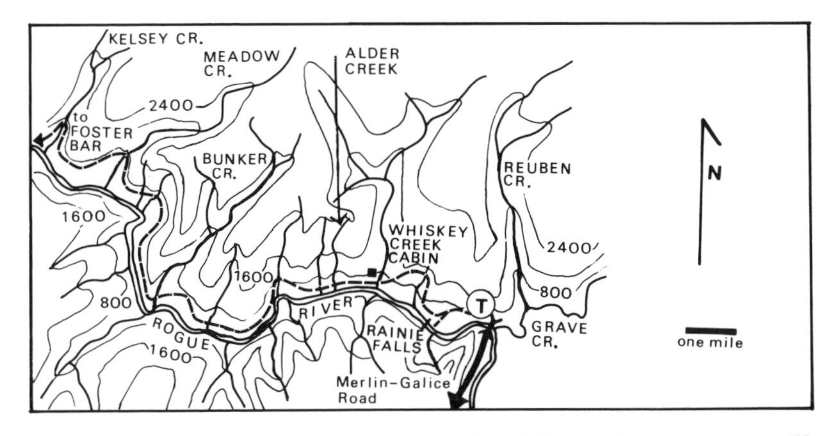

The trail, of good width and grade, follows the canyon wall about 100 feet above the Rogue. Myrtle, live oak, and poison oak are well represented, but the poison oak does not encroach on the trail. At 1.4 miles, the hiker passes a "High Water" sign indicating the mark where the Rogue crested in December 1964, some 55 feet above its summer level. Throughout the journey, the Rogue is a captivating guide.

At 2.1 miles, the trail splits. The trail downhill to the left leads to Rainie Falls and a campsite. During late summer, the arched backs of salmon break the water's surface as they struggle against the current. But the best views of Rainie Falls are secured from the south bank.

By China Gulch, the trail is well above the river. Arms of madrone and oak interlace, forming a canopy over the trail. More trees separate the hiker from the river.

A large riverside camp marks Whiskey Creek. Where the trail crosses the bridge, a side trail leads to Whiskey Cabin (100 yards). The cabin supports a host of outbuildings, an abandoned apple orchard, and some rusting remnants from its heyday.

At 4.5 miles, there is a campsite that caters more to the hiker than the rafter. Located on an inland bench, the site enjoys the tranquility of a madrone–cedar–pine forest. An ash woodland signals Alder Creek in .5 mile.

At 8.7 miles, the trail passes Slim Pickens, a narrow passage of the river.

From Bunker Creek, the trail climbs. More firs, maples, and myrtles enter the vegetation mix. The view grows restricted with the filling in of the forest. At 14 miles, there's an inviting campsite with tables and grills near Copsey Creek. A side trail leads down to the Rogue.

At 17.5 miles, Kelsey Creek beckons with its deep swimming holes. River rafters camped on the sandy bar below often hike up

Western fence lizard

to this retreat. About 50 yards from Kelsey Creek, the trail again splits. Take the branch leading down to the river. The river now widens—its broad green back a hypnotic guide.

Approaching Ditch Creek, the trail winds through an ash–oak-studded grassland above the river. As the next stretch of trail can be hot and dry, top off the water jugs.

At 20 miles and again at 20.9 miles, slides have blocked the original trail. The Bureau of Land Management has constructed temporary inland detours, until scheduled funding allows for the stabilization and improvement of the original trail. The detours, however, take the trail away from the private property where Zane Grey's Cabin stands.

At Quail Creek the trail approaches a wide sandy bar on the river, ideal for cooling one's feet and enjoying the beauty of the Rogue. Where the trail crosses Quail Creek, follow the branch that retraces the creek back toward the river. The trail meets briefly with an old road, then it resumes with a steep inland climb to skirt another slide. Young firs cover the slope, interrupted by some mighty madrones.

At 23.7 miles, the trail enters the Quail Creek fire zone. This human-caused fire of 1970 jumped the river, scorching both banks and burning 2800 acres.

At Rogue River Ranch, the trail forks. The branch uphill to the right leads to the ranch and the continuation of the trail. (The lower trail leads to the campsites.) But by cutting across Mule Creek below the ranch, you can avoid between 1 and 1.5 road miles. Eventually, though, the trail along the Rogue dies. After climbing the bank and meeting the forest road, take a left.

Instead of this shortcut, you may explore the grounds and enter the designated buildings of the Rogue River Ranch, which is still undergoing restoration. Pamphlets, identifying the structures and telling the story, are available on site.

From the ranch, the main trail meets with the road from Marial at 27.7 miles. Stay left, crossing the bridge over Mule Creek. Make sure the water jugs are full before leaving the creek (use a filter, of course). When the trail returns to the river, it traces a hot, dry course along a basalt bench, with limited vegetation for shade.

Continuing along the road, the route enters Siskiyou National Forest and passes the Mule Creek Guard Station. From the station, the trail proper resumes in .6 mile, soon entering the Wild Rogue Wilderness.

The trail approaches the river where it narrows. At 30.2 miles, views of the churning Coffeepot catch the hiker's attention. Coffeepot marks the narrowest passage on the Rogue. In .5 mile, a waterfall spills into the Rogue from its canyon on the south bank. From the elevated course, vistas are grand, but the heat-radiating basalt speeds the step of the summertime hiker.

The basalt bench signals an overall character change for the trail, as it abandons its undulating, inland forest pursuit.

Greeting the hot and weary at 32.5 miles are Burns and Blossom Bar creeks. The alder-lined banks of the latter shade its deep, shimmery pools.

After traveling through the meadow posted "Wild Turkey Enhancement Area," the hiker arrives at Paradise Lodge, homesteaded in 1907. It offers a pleasing rest stop and such creature comforts as iced drinks. The wide sweeping lawns are playground to the lodge's tame deer.

To return to the trail, travel uphill from the lodge, pass through the gate, and walk up the grassy runway strip. The trail begins in the trees at the runway's top. It then follows a rocky cliff above the Rogue before delivering the hiker to the flat woodland of Brushy Bar. Brushy Bar offers ample camping opportunity, but its creek is unreliable.

From the bar, the trail climbs to the sign noting Captain Tichenor's defeat. In 1856, Indians halted Tichenor's rescue of the Illahe settlers by rolling rocks down this steep embankment, disbanding the troops.

Near Clay Hill Creek, the hiker encounters more private residences. The trail draws away from the river.

At 42.5 miles, Flora Dell Creek beckons with its 30-foot waterfall. The occasional roar of a jet boat operating between Foster Bar and Paradise Lodge shatters the calm and interrupts the wilderness experience.

The summer sun takes a harsher toll on the creeks along the final stretch of trail. While there's water for filling jugs, there aren't the tempting pools of the creeks lying farther east. River access is limited.

Leaving Billings Creek, the trail snakes through and around the ranchland property of Big Bend Pasture before delivering the hiker to the Foster Bar trailhead and the close of an unforgettable hike.

39 LOWER ROGUE RIVER

Distance: 12.2 miles (car shuttle)
Elevation Change: 600 feet
Difficulty: Strenuous
Maps: USGS Agness and Collier Butte; USFS Siskiyou National Forest
Water: Rogue River and its tributaries (purification recommended)
Season: All year (in winter, call about road conditions)
For More Information: Gold Beach Ranger District

This trail tours the Rogue River segment bearing the designation "scenic." Under the Wild and Scenic River Act of 1968, three designations were described: wild, scenic, and recreational. By definition, a "scenic" river is both unimpounded and largely undeveloped, although it is accessible. A "wild" river is more primitive, a "recreational" river more developed.

But the scenic qualities of this river segment far exceed the basic requirements of the designation. Snaking through the

Lower Rogue River

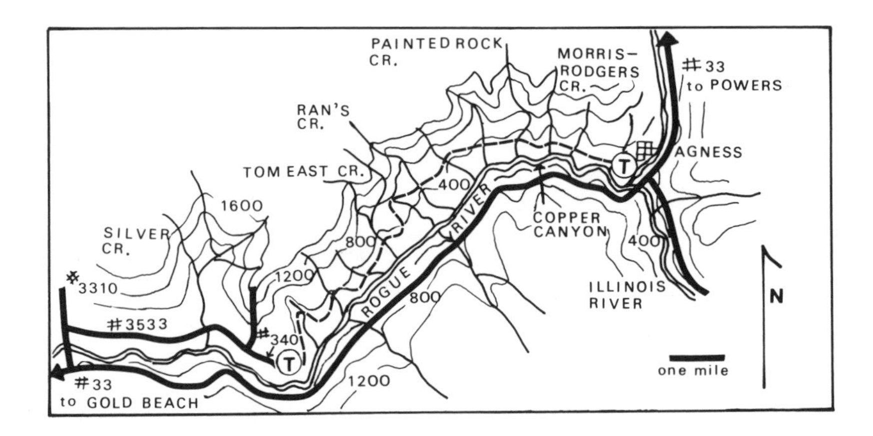

rugged terrain of the coastal mountains, the river and its companion trail introduce the hiker to a diverse floral community. Lush fern canyons, myrtle–tanoak woodlands, black huckleberry-crowded hillsides, and stands of Douglas fir and western red cedar highlight this trail of many faces.

The hiker finds microenvironments that call to mind the rain forest of the Olympic Peninsula and the chaparral akin to southern and central California. More than a dozen cascading creeks punctuate the floral diversity.

Historically, the bounty of this area attracted Indian fishing parties, trappers, prospectors, and settlers. Today, that bounty attracts the hiker.

To reach the Agness Trailhead from Gold Beach, take Forest SR 33 east to Agness (about 30 miles). At the northwest end of Agness, there's a junction near a little market. Take the road indicated as a dead end, following it west to its close. The trailhead is located directly across from the Agness Post Office. Parking for the trailhead is located at the Community Library, .2 mile back on this road.

To reach the west trailhead from Gold Beach, travel 10 miles east on Forest SR 33. Turn north onto Forest SR 3310, crossing over the Rogue River. In .25 mile take a right onto Forest SR 3533. A mile after the Silver Creek bridge, the road branches. Stay on Forest SR 3533, following signs to the trail. Where the road again branches in less than 1 mile, a right leads onto Forest SR 3533.340. This marks the beginning of a narrow one-lane road. In .3 mile, take a left uphill and proceed .1 mile to Parking Area #1, .25 mile to Parking Area #2. The trailhead is located across from Parking Area #1. All roads are passable with conventional vehicles.

Beginning from the Agness Trailhead, the trail crosses over

Rilea Creek to arrive at a T junction. Here the trail (now a road) turns left and passes through farmhouse property. Be sure to leave the gates as they were found. The road then climbs, with the trail proper resuming in .1 mile on the right.

The many creeks that slice the trail are natural gauges of distance. Near Rilea Creek, the Forest Service has posted signs warning that some of the bridges are in disrepair. Here, as elsewhere, funding limitations have hindered proper trail maintenance.

At a half mile, the hiker arrives at Briar Creek, the first of a series. After Briar Creek, the trail works its way back toward the river through a myrtle–tanoak woodland.

The often deciduous-lined trail introduces seasonal drama to the Rogue. Winter brings open vistas and a leaf-matted trail, spring and summer a rustling skyline. In early morning, the rolling frolic of the river otters may amuse the shoreline visitor.

The level floor of the myrtle grove offers campsite potential. Easy river access is a plus for these sites.

At 1.4 miles, the trail charges uphill, delivering the hiker to a dirt road. An osprey nest atop a snag can be seen just prior to reaching the road. The trail heads left, crossing the Blue Jay Creek bridge, then bears right per the sign.

Throughout its 12.2 miles, the trail is fairly well marked, but one trouble spot occurs just after Smithers Creek bridge. A few yards beyond the creek, the Lower Rogue Trail branches to the right. By appearance, this would seem a secondary trail, but the well-trampled trail ahead leads to a private residence. A rock cairn and/or a trail sign (somewhat hidden from the path) indicate the junction.

At 2.6 miles, Copper Canyon's rocky outpost delivers an overlook of the Rogue River. This elevated post provides the best river vistas of the hike. It's an inviting place for a rest and a snack. It is also the most exposed section of the hike if it's rainy or windy.

"Bagging" creeks, at 3.1 miles the hiker arrives at Painted Rock Creek. Leo, Stonehouse, Spring, and Sundown creeks follow, any one of which offers an invitation to linger. Ran's Creek (listed as Bridge Creek on the topo) marks the halfway point.

Lush sword-fern canyons house these creeks. In the winter and spring, the pulsing waterways steal the show. In summertime, it's the greenery that's special.

If a car shuttle does not present itself as an option, Ran's Creek is a good break-off point for day hiking from either trailhead.

The ridge between Ran's Creek and Schoolhouse Creek marks the highest elevation of the trek (752 feet). Leaving Schoolhouse Creek (at 6.7 miles) the trail now is more exposed and remains so until Tom East Creek (7.9 miles). At 7.4 miles, after crossing an inclined bridge, the hiker approaches a burned-out shed (the John Adams place, burned in 1958). In the grassy field 100 feet west of the shed, one obtains a good river vista, overlooking the clearcut hillside of a private property.

The trail resumes on the road to the left. Midway, a stubborn gate cuts the road.

The creeks along this west segment of trail offer the easiest paths to the river. The trail itself follows an elevated course along the bank.

From Auberry Creek (8.7 miles) to Slide Creek (11 miles), the trail assumes an even course. Rhododendron drapes the trail leaving Slide Creek. The final leg offers a steady ascent to Forest SR 3533.340, climbing out of the deciduous forest and traveling through an open area punctuated by mature Douglas fir to arrive at the trailhead.

40 GRASSY KNOB WILDERNESS

Distance: 2 miles round trip
Elevation Change: 400 feet
Difficulty: Easy
Maps: USGS Port Orford and Langlois; USFS Siskiyou National Forest
Water: Carry water
Season: All year
For More Information: Powers Ranger District

Grassy Knob (elevation 2342 feet) was the one-time site of a lookout tower. Today, some broken glass from the tower's dismantling litters the knob. Young Douglas fir and scrub oak have begun to encroach on the vantage point, but the panorama remains worthwhile, with views of Port Orford, Cape Blanco, Humbug Mountain State Park, Bald Mountain, and Rocky Peak.

The soothing face of the Pacific and the ceaseless ridges, knobs, and knolls of the Coast Range provide for a scenic, tranquil visit.

Hemlock, Douglas fir, myrtle, and rhododendron line the "trail" (formerly a road) that leads to Grassy Knob Wilderness. The size and quality of the road indicate how close we came to losing this wild land.

With the primary management goal being fish protection, there are no plans for additional trails within the wilderness at this time. However, the Forest Service is considering building a trail between Grassy Knob and China Peak to the north.

Humbug Mountain in the distance, from Grassy Knob Summit

Grassy Knob holds the distinction of being the only mainland site where Americans fired on enemy Japanese aircraft during World War II.

To reach the wilderness from U.S. 101, hikers turn east onto Grassy Knob Road (located just south of the Cape Blanco State Park turnoff). The road is paved for the first 4 miles, then turns to gravel. At the gate at 4.4 miles, the road becomes Forest SR 5105. The trailhead is at the end of the road, 7.9 miles from U.S. 101.

The road is passable with conventional vehicles, but the angled drainage furrows create effective speed bumps. Trailhead parking is on the right.

The Grassy Knob Trail begins at the guard rail at the end of Forest SR 5105. Following the gravel road (now the trail), the hiker gains overviews of the wilderness, but the wide cut of the

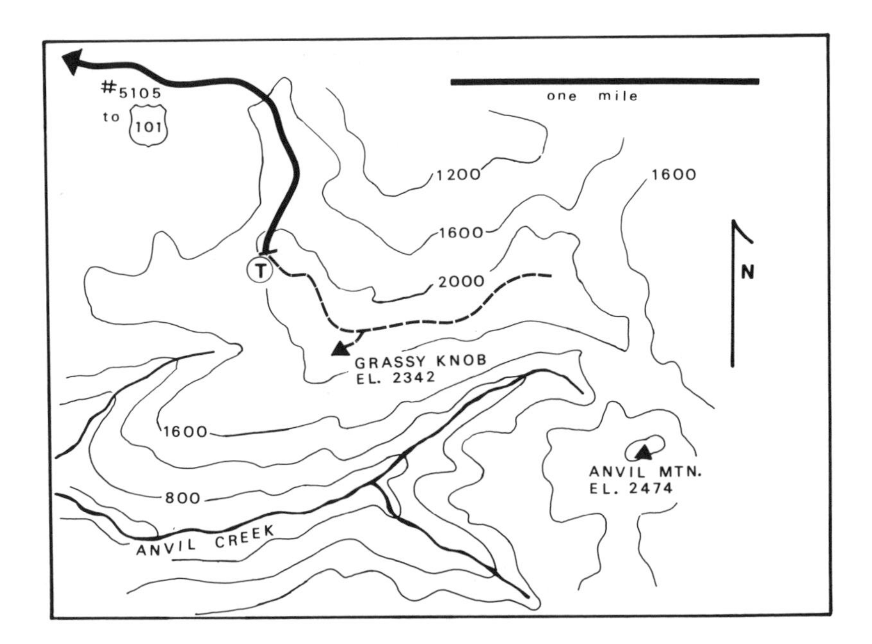

roadbed denies close-up viewing of small plants. Lupine and some hardy grasses and seedlings have begun to break through the gravel trailbed, but much more time is needed to reduce its road-like appearance. Grassy Knob's southern location introduces variety to the plant complex, joining wet-forest and dry-forest plant species.

Where the road curves and widens at the top of the first hill (.3 mile), there is an open grassy slope to the hiker's right (south). Heading up the slope, the hiker will notice some discarded wood and metal containers. From here, one spies the trail leading to the right. This is the footpath to Grassy Knob, 100 yards ahead. The name is a misnomer, for Grassy Knob is actually a rocky outpost. And there's no clue that the knob ever supported a grassy top.

The summit offers eye-catching views of the coast, Humbug Mountain, and the surrounding Coast Range. It's a peaceful location in which to absorb the morning rays or watch the setting of the sun. The wide trailbed allows for a safe return trip to the vehicle at dusk.

Continuing east on the redesignated road offers additional vistas of the wilderness and the coastline to the south. Giant rhododendron, Douglas fir, hemlock, and scrub oak line the road-trail. At 1 mile, this introduction to the wilderness ends at a rounded turnout. Further exploration requires cross-country skills.

41 ILLINOIS RIVER NATIONAL RECREATION TRAIL

Distance: 16.4 miles round trip
Elevation Change: 900 feet
Difficulty: Strenuous
Maps: USGS Agness, Collier Butte, and Pearsoll Peak; USFS Siskiyou National Forest or Kalmiopsis Wilderness/Wild Rogue Wilderness
Water: Illinois River tributaries
Season: Spring through fall (in winter, call regarding snow on roads and trail)
For More Information: Galice Ranger District or Gold Beach Ranger District

Concluding at Silver Creek, this trail travels 8.2 miles of the 27-mile Illinois River National Recreation Trail. It travels an elevated course above the Wild and Scenic River. The steep, rugged terrain prohibits a closer acquaintance with this wide-backed beauty. Still, frequent glimpses secured through the varied tree cover of madrone, live oak, cedar and fir, along with select, limited approaches, are found along the trail's course.

The many side creeks alone are inducement to tour this trail. Lined by bigleaf maple, alder, and myrtle, the creeks charm the visitor with cascades of white swirling water and moss-capped rocks. The force of the water fans the neighboring maidenhair ferns into a dancing display.

The rock outcrop, Buzzards Roost (elevation 1146 feet), affords the prized vistas of this hike. With a fairly easy climb to a rocky saddle, the hiker secures views of the Illinois River and its broad sweeping valley to the west. A more difficult climb to the top is necessary to view the upstream waters of the Illinois River.

The lightning fires of August 30, 1987, which burned 96,540 acres in the Silver Complex, lightly touched this trail. Where Silver Peak displays patches of fire-bronzed trees, the trailside damage is limited to brief areas of charred trunks amid a singed understory. Just three months following the fire, new moss and green foliage spattered the fire-darkened ground, promising a rapid regeneration of the forest. In coming years, springtime hikers should find a floral bonanza.

To reach this trail from U.S. 101 in Gold Beach, turn east on South Bank Road (County 595), which later becomes Forest SR 33. In 27 miles, a turn right leads onto Forest SR 450, the narrow, winding road indicated for the Illinois River Trail, Oak Flat, and Game Lake Trail. The trailhead is to the left in 3.2 miles. There's a vault toilet at the parking area for visitor convenience.

The trail climbs the bench above the Illinois River. Myrtle and madrone weave through the fir, with sword fern, moss, and tanoak puncturing the leaf mat. Where the trail draws closer to the edge of the bench, tree-filtered views of the green-flowing Illinois greet the hiker. Mighty madrone cling to the steeply dropping slope. Old fence posts and time-worn fences attest to homestead efforts.

At .7 mile, the trail arrives at Nancy Creek. Here, a secondary trail that requires fording departs to the right. The main trail continues uphill another .1 mile to the Nancy Creek bridge and more intimate views of the tumbling waters.

The secondary trail rejoins the main trail at 1 mile, after touring an open slope dotted by cedar. The main trail tours a moister region and sports a border thick with black huckleberry.

Except during times of drought, several smaller creeks (not indicated on the maps) cross the trail, offering a chance to replenish the water supply. (Note: Today, all drinking water should be purified.)

From Ethel's Creek, at 1.5 miles, the trail climbs to Buzzards Roost at 2.25 miles. Here, the hiker secures a vantage on the Illinois River Valley. This trip is ideal for a short day hike.

The niches of Buzzards Roost create a gallery for the area vegetation. Manzanita, madrone, myrtle, live oak, tanoak, fir, and pine all take refuge in the rock, yet do not infringe on the vista.

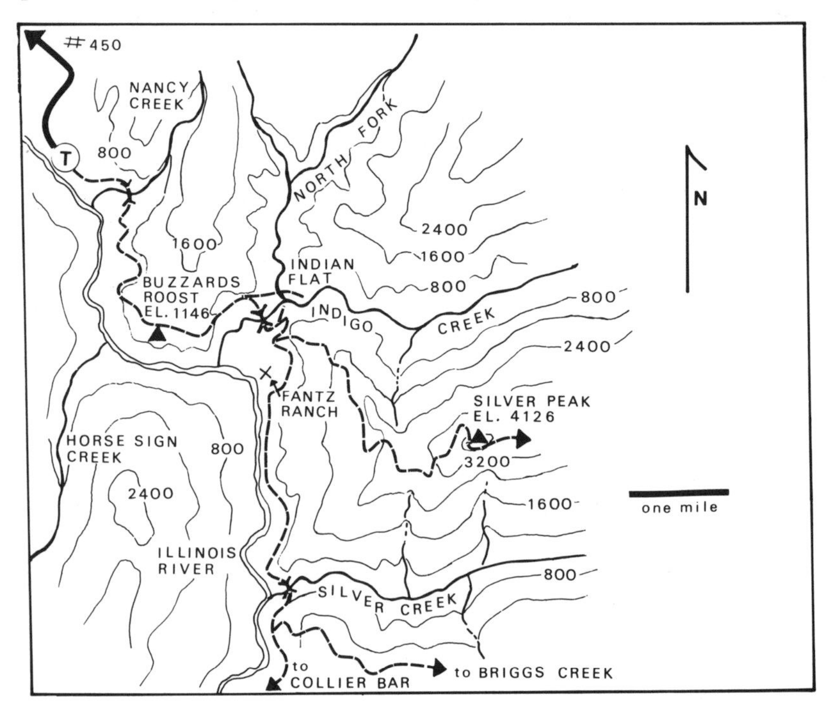

Indigo Creek

As the trail winds downhill to the Indian Flat junction, the hiker secures views of Silver Peak, with its bald top and fire-bronzed patches.

At the junction at 3.7 miles, going straight leads to Indian Flat in a quarter mile. This broad, open grassland, punctuated by mature evergreens and patches of myrtle, offers prized campsites and easy access to Indigo Creek.

Taking a right at the junction leads to the continuation of the Illinois River Trail. The bridge crossing at Indigo Creek is a welcome sight, as the milky green waters squeeze through the canyon, forming rapid chutes and deep pools. On the rock walls, olive-green mosses offer contrast.

Climbing above Indigo Creek, the trail veers into the fire zone. About 200 feet from the bridge, a side trail to the left leads to a large, established campsite. A rocky bar separates the camp from the creek's edge.

Indigo Creek is a sensitive area for pine marten and other indicator species. As such, it proved an important study site for the salvage effort following the fires.

At 4.5 miles, the trail draws to the top of the ridge (elevation 814 feet). Here, the Hobson–Silver Peak Trail branches to the left. Along it, the hiker may notice evidence of helicopter logging, part of the salvage effort.

The trail continues downhill, leaving behind evidence of the fire. The owner of the upcoming ranch has posted trailside signs cautioning dog owners to leash their pets. Please respect the rights of local residents, and insure continued public access to the trail.

Nearing Fantz Ranch (also referred to as Briggs Ranch), the trailside habitat grows more bountiful with groves of bigleaf maple and oak, tangles of black huckleberry, and some stout fir.

At 5 miles, there's an area set aside on the ranch for campers, with the provision that they notify the owner of their presence. Crossing Coon Creek, the trail tours a steeper slope dressed mainly in live oak.

After only snatches of Illinois River scenics, the hiker secures unimpeded viewing of the river at 6.5 miles. Belted kingfishers and ospreys patrol the waters. On hot summer days, the river is indeed a temptress—inviting, yet unapproachable.

Beyond Bluff Creek, the trail detours around a landslide. With the steep terrain, tree falls and slides plague the trail, but the maintenance is first-rate.

At 7.25 miles, the trail enters the Kalmiopsis Wilderness. A large, open meadow welcomes the hiker. Campsites are found in the trees ringing the meadow.

At the Silver Creek confluence, hikers earn exciting views of the Illinois River. At 8.2 miles, this hike concludes at Silver Creek.

Landslides complicated by ice halted our winter exploration, a fact of off-season hiking. But normally, the hiker can continue exploring the northern boundary of the Kalmiopsis Wilderness, journeying over Bald Mountain and traveling through the York Creek Botanical Area to Briggs Creek for a 27-mile one-way distance.

An alternative hike is to take the trail to Collier Bar at the junction in .5 mile. The Collier Bar Trail pursues the Illinois River south for a 10-mile one-way distance from Oak Flat. At Collier Bar, the hiker must ford the Illinois River to reach the bench campsite.

42 BIGELOW LAKES-BOUNDARY TRAIL (NORTH)

Distance: 17 miles round trip to Windy Gap
Elevation Change: 1200 feet; course characterized by dips and climbs
Difficulty: Strenuous
Maps: USGS Oregon Caves; USFS Siskiyou National Forest
Water: Springs (purification required)
Season: Spring through fall
For More Information: Illinois Valley Ranger District

See map on page 147.

This trail lies well inland, yet it earns its coastal designation. On a hot summer day, the temperature inversion summons swirling veils of ocean mist to this distant mountain post.

Lowland meadows brimming with false hellebore and high mountain meadows painted in springtime punctuate the rising-dipping course of the Bigelow Lakes-Boundary Trail. Manzanita and cedar intersperse the fir–spruce forest. In the 1980s, the trail's scenic qualities and its rising popularity easily won it the nod for National Recreation Trail distinction.

As a conclusion to the northward discovery of this trail, Windy Gap is ideal. This outpost provides riveting views of imposing

False hellebore

Grayback Mountain (elevation 7055 feet), the patchwork beauty of the Williams Valley, and the reigning presence of Mt. Shasta and Mt. McLoughlin. Not even the wind can dissuade a lingering visit. For many of the locals, this is an annual trek.

To reach this trail from the junction of U.S. 199 and Oregon 46 in Cave Junction, take Oregon 46 east, following the signs to Oregon Caves National Monument. After 13.5 miles on Oregon 46, turn left (north) onto Forest SR 4613, a good gravel road. After 6.6 miles, turn right onto Bigelow Lakes Road (Forest SR 070).

The road is marked "Limited Maintenance, Not Suitable for Low Clearance Vehicles," but it remains in good condition. After .7 mile on Forest SR 070, bear right. The trailhead is in 1.3 miles, with roadside turnouts for parking. The best opportunities for parking lie on the opposite side of the gate.

The trail shares its first 2.5 miles with Hike 43, tracing a zigzag course to the saddle of Lake and Elijah mountains before charging downhill to a large open campsite and the beginning of the Boundary Trail.

The trail segment to Windy Gap departs the northeast end of the campsite. It immediately cuts through a field of false hellebore, then parallels a row of bushes at the base of the meadow. Deer, grouse, and brightly colored western tanagers often highlight the trek.

Following a general northeast course, in .25 mile the hiker finds the springs that service the campsite. From here, the trail alternately divides meadowland and traces the forest edge. This open stretch of trail can be hot going, so carry extra water.

At 3.5 miles, in the center of a meadow, there's a Windy Gap–Bolan Lookout mileage marker in disrepair. To the left, across the meadow, lies the Elk Creek Trail, and to its left are campsites, secluded in the trees. The route continues straight.

The Boundary Trail now makes a serious assault on the unnamed peak (elevation 6418 feet) identified on the Oregon Caves topo. A quick scramble off the trail reaches the summit. Awaiting is 360-degree viewing of the surrounding area.

Leaving the unnamed peak, the trail follows an undulating course toward Grayback Mountain. Manzanita and some cedar enter the forest complex.

On the saddle below Grayback, the outline of the trail grows faint. Two footpaths can be discerned. One, heading off to the left, is the path of choice; the second disappears into the trees on the right.

As the trail enters a grassland, at 7 miles, it again fades. Proceeding through that grassland, the hiker comes upon a sign for Cold Springs and an area sheep camp. Head uphill to the left toward Cold Springs to continue the journey to Windy Gap.

Cold Springs is the largest spring encountered along the trail. It also marks the end of shade. Carry plenty of water for the dusty climb to Windy Gap.

A grassy meadow rippled by the wind commands the next stretch of trail. Indian paintbrush, yarrow, bog orchids, and tiny yellow monkey flowers interrupt the flowing blades of green.

Trailside, a boulder overlook affords views of the valley and Krause Cabin, a former line cabin for livestock management. Windy Gap awaits on the horizon.

At 7.5 miles, the hiker arrives at a trail junction and another mileage marker for the Boundary Trail. The size of this sign defies the souvenir collector.

Windy Gap

The trail then continues along the slope, before charging to Windy Gap (8.5 miles). The steepness of the trail has left its bed heavily furrowed.

Atop Windy, the panorama showcases Mt. McLoughlin to the east, Mt. Shasta to the southeast, Grayback to the south, and the patchwork scheme of the Williams Creek Valley to the northeast.

Sugarloaf lies on the far side of Windy, to the left of the trail as the hiker approaches the gap. There's but a faint trail to the top of Sugarloaf. A steep, rugged trail to the Williams area descends from the north side of the gap.

Return the way you came.

43 BIGELOW LAKES-BOUNDARY TRAIL (SOUTH)

Distance: 16 miles round trip to Swan Mountain Saddle
Elevation Change: 1000 feet; course characterized by dips and climbs
Difficulty: Strenuous
Maps: USGS Oregon Caves; USFS Siskiyou National Forest
Water: Springs (purification required)
Season: Spring through fall
For More Information: Illinois Valley Ranger District

The Boundary Trail component of this hike won National Recreation Trail distinction in the 1980s. It snakes along the outreaches of Oregon Caves National Monument and the Rogue River National Forest, before dipping into the Red Buttes Wilderness.

The secluded off-trail beauty of Bigelow Lakes introduces and closes this hike. A mosaic of lily pads decorates each lake.

The trail takes the hiker on a roller-coaster trek, over saddles and ridges and through valleys. Among the sidelights is the time-touched presence of Denman Cabin, a one-time line shack for livestock management. The cabin is a rustic spot for a midday meal.

Vistas are obtained throughout the journey. But an off-trail excursion to the top of Craggy Mountain unfolds a spectacle. Craggy offers a 360-degree introduction to the neighborhood: Little Craggy Peak, Swan Mountain, and the Sucker Creek drainage, along with Elijah, Lake, and Grayback mountains. Piercing the horizon are Mt. Shasta, and Mt. McLoughlin, and California's Pyramid Peak.

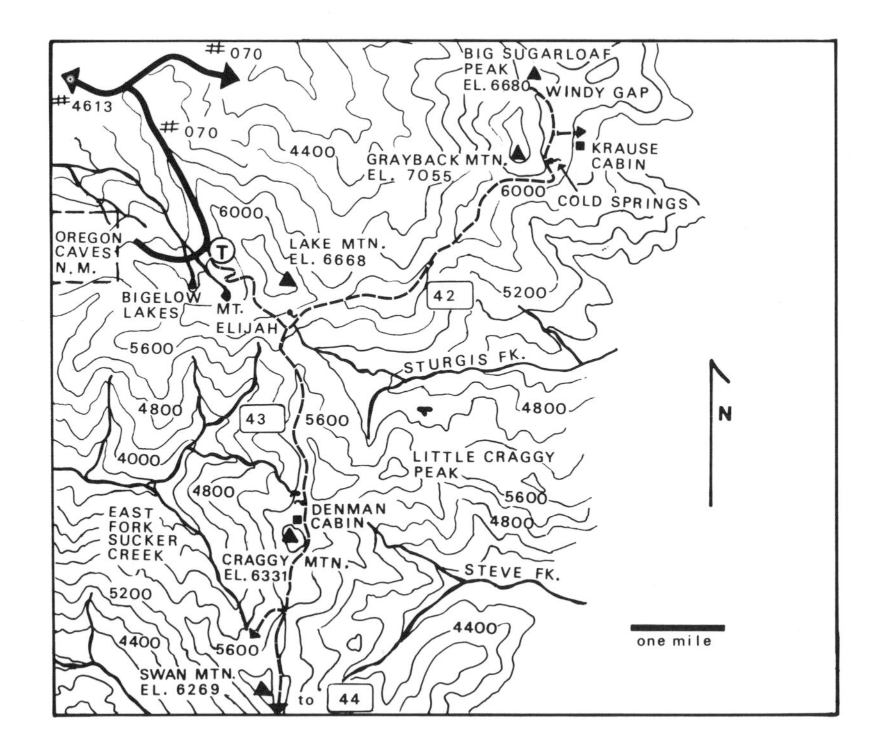

Directions to the trailhead are the same as those for Hike 42, Bigelow Lakes—Boundary Trail (North). The trail begins climbing in zigzag fashion between two wide sweeps of mountain meadow. At .6 mile, a signpost, denuded of sign, marks a footpath striking out across the west meadow. The path fades, but following its general course delivers the hiker to a gated fence, with the larger Bigelow Lake lying just beyond. Cows graze this land, necessitating the fence.

False hellebore, yarrow, Indian paintbrush, aster, daisy, and lupine color the tall, wind-bowed grasses of the meadow. Lichen-etched granitoid rocks and boulders dot its surface.

The main trail continues climbing, offering overviews of Bigelow Lake, its feeding waters, and the ridges fanning to the horizon. The rocky slopes carry the delicate ornamentation of yellow paintbrush and flowering succulents.

At 1.5 miles, the trail arrives at the saddle bridging Lake Mountain and Mt. Elijah (named for the discoverer of Oregon Caves). Again, the signs are missing. The trail heading downhill connects to the Boundary Trail, while the trail striking out to the right leads to Mt. Elijah, Oregon Caves, and Hike 45. Backtracking 50 yards on Bigelow Lakes Trail, find the unmarked branch

Bigelow Lake

to Lake Mountain, angling off to the northeast.

Continue downhill to the Boundary Trail junction and a large campsite at 2.5 miles. With a spring to the northeast, this campsite is the ideal base from which to explore both directions of the Boundary Trail (see Hike 42).

To tour the southern segment of this trail, exit the southeast end of the campsite. From here, the trail ascends. It's mostly shaded beneath the fir–spruce canopy. Tanoak, vanilla leaf, and twisted stalk add to the understory. At 3.4 miles, the trail enters Elkhorn Prairie. Columbine, larkspur, pink paintbrush, and a variety of tall flowers crowd the edges of the trail.

Just prior to the saddle, at 4.7 miles, is Horse Camp Springs. Crossing the saddle, the hiker first glimpses the destinations east. Steller's jays, hawks, woodpeckers, and grouse abound, so keep the binoculars handy.

A brief walk brings the hiker to an unmarked trail junction. Traveling uphill to the right leads to the collapsing shell of Denman Cabin and an enticing, though nonpotable spring in .1 mile. From the cabin, a trail crosses over the spring, and eventually rejoins the main trail. Staying on the Boundary Trail, it rounds the east flank of Craggy Mountain.

To stage a cross-country assault on Craggy's summit, head up the south slope. On top, a prized vista awaits. Mt. Shasta and Mt.

McLoughlin, the southern Siskiyous, and the distant Cascades display wilderness grandeur. Solitude reigns.

At 6.5 miles, the main trail meets the East Fork Sucker Creek Trail on the Craggy–Swan Mountain saddle. From here, the Boundary Trail travels through dry forest, before slicing the lush meadow that earns Green Valley its name.

From Green Valley, it's an uphill climb to the Swan Mountain saddle (8 miles), the stopping point for this hike. The Boundary Trail does however continue south, eventually becoming part of the Red Buttes Wilderness trail system (Hike 44).

As a closing destination, the Swan Mountain Saddle offers rewarding views of Tannen Mountain, Sucker Butte, and Red Buttes Wilderness. The saddle itself is wind-whipped, dry meadowland. To achieve the summit vantage requires a half-mile cross-country effort.

Return as you came.

44 RED BUTTES WILDERNESS

Distance: 16 miles round trip
Elevation Change: 2300 feet
Difficulty: Strenuous
Maps: USGS Oregon Caves; USFS Siskiyou National Forest
Water: Various sources as indicated on USGS maps; not all springs are reliable (purify all drinking water)
Season: Spring through fall
For More Information: Illinois Valley Ranger District

The Red Buttes Wilderness trail system features the finest vistas in the coastal mountains of Southern Oregon. Situated on the California–Oregon border, the wilderness ridges offer riveting views of both states. Mt. Shasta and Mt. McLoughlin, Pyramid Peak, Grayback Mountain, and the Crater Lake region headline the attractions.

Introducing the trail system, Tannen Lake and East Tannen Lake invite the unburdening of the pack. Set in a bowl, each reflects rock-studded slopes and billowing alders. Silver, weathered logs bump against the shoreline.

A side attraction to the trail is Fosters Temple. Aptly named, this cedar sports a fire-hollowed center, a knothole admitting light, and a lichen-etched doorway.

To tour the trail system from the junction of U.S. 199 and Oregon 46 in Cave Junction, travel south on U.S. 199 for 6.4

miles. Take a left on the road indicated for "Waldo, Takilma, and Happy Camp," just north of O'Brien. At the stop sign in 4.8 miles, the route proceeds straight ahead toward Bolan Lake. About 12 miles from the stop sign, turn left onto Forest SR 4812, a one-lane gravel road with turnouts. There's a sign at this turn for Bolan and Tannen lakes. Travel 4 miles; then turn right onto Forest SR 4812.041. The Tannen Lake trailhead lies ahead in 4.7 miles. The parking turnout lies another 100 yards down the road.

The trail enters Red Buttes Wilderness, striping the slope on the southside of Forest SR 4812.041. Tanoak, snowberry, Prince's pine, strawberry, thimbleberry, and more unite in an explosion of green. Firs stand sentinel over the trail, with cedars and spruce infiltrating the ranks.

A meadow brimming with bracken fern and pearly everlasting announces Tannen Lake. Where the trail forks, the branch uphill to the right leads to Sundown Gap. The main trail continues through the meadow to the lake.

Tannen Lake offers three lakeside camps, with a fourth site just up the hill from the crossing of Tannen Creek. Alders and willows rim the lake, with some stout Douglas firs for neighbors. Rock outcrops and chutes interrupt the tree scatter and low vegetation of the slope. The trail continues, crossing a rickety duckboard over Tannen Creek.

East Tannen Lake (1 mile) presents a face similar to that of the first lake, save for the rocky summit of Tannen Mountain peeking over its bowl. The border of East Tannen is more overgrown, denying lakeside camping save for one small informal site.

The trail pulls away from the lake, rounding its north end and migrating east. Rocks and boulders add to the wilderness setting, as a few weeping spruce enter the forest complex. Soon, a side trail climbing from the road joins the trail.

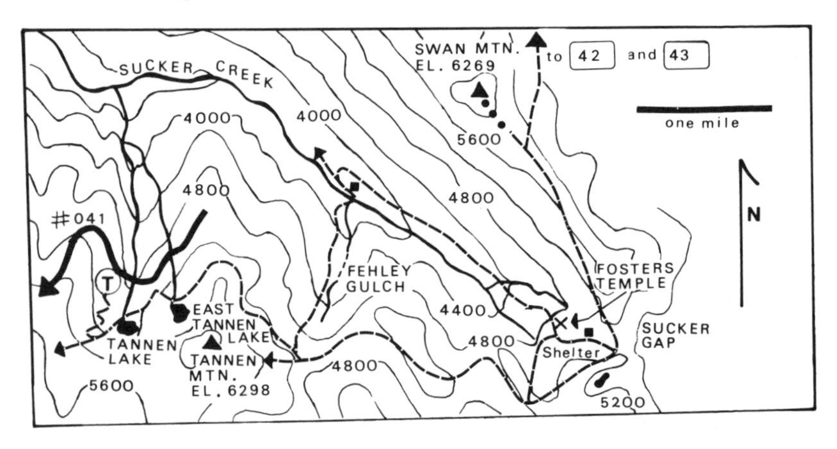

Swan Mountain

As the main trail mounts the rocky slope, views of Swan Mountain and Fehley Gulch address the hiker. Ahead at 3 miles lies a trail junction. Follow the Fehley Gulch Trail, which angles back to the left, to begin a clockwise tour of the loop.

Early on, the trail is but faintly defined. But beyond the first switchback, with its presiding stand of world-class cedar, frequent sign placements confirm the trail's presence. Approaching Fehley Gulch, the trail gains definition.

At 4.5 miles, the trail crosses Fehley Gulch and Sucker Creek. Springtime hikers will find a wet crossing. Where the trail crosses Fehley Gulch, there's a mining claim with some rocker boxes.

Leaving Sucker Creek, the trail passes the site of a former cabin. The foundation has been cleared for a campsite, but beware of stray nails and glass. Past the site is a trail junction. A right turn toward Sucker Gap continues the loop.

Once past the New Dawn placer claim, the trail charges up the slope, reaching a grass and bracken fern meadow. Young cedars have reclaimed the meadow fringes. The trail continues climbing, bypassing Fosters Temple. Orange-painted arrows on a trailside tree point out this attraction.

In a short distance, some signs in disrepair greet the hiker. Just past these signs, the trail comes to a T. A left leads to Sucker Gap, the shelter, Swan Mountain, and the continuation of the loop. A right leads to the Boundary Trail in .25 mile for an abbreviated loop.

Taking a left, the hiker passes through a cedar grouping to a second meadow. A large cedar with double orange striping marks the trail entry. Tracing an even course through the meadow, the hiker rediscovers the trail to the shelter and Sucker Gap, just below the spring. The shelter lies beyond the tree border at 6.7 miles.

Bypassing the shelter, the hiker may climb the heavily eroded trail, journeying up through the second meadow to Sucker Gap Trail.

The shelter, however, offers a clean retreat. Its partial wooden floor welcomes bed rolls. A spring lies on the Sucker Gap Trail uphill and to the right from the shelter, should the springs in the nearby meadow prove dry.

From the shelter, the trail climbs to the gap and the Boundary Trail junction (7 miles). Here, Swan Mountain beckons for a brief detour from the loop.

The Swan Mountain detour follows the Boundary Trail toward Bigelow Lakes, touring the pine-dotted gap meadow, before climbing through a mixed conifer forest void of groundcover.

On this comfortably graded course, the hiker churns away the mileage, while the trail's sameness inspires mental ramblings. Where the trail breaks into the open, manzanita and buckwheat dress the ridge.

On the Swan Mountain saddle, at 8.6 miles, the Boundary Trail heads down to Green Valley and destinations north, Hikes 43 and 42.

To conquer the summit, it is a .5-mile cross-country scramble. Trail fragments aid the hiker in picking a path around and through the manzanita. A couple of false summits add to the anticipation.

The top of Swan Mountain presents 360-degree viewing of Mt. Shasta and Mt. McLoughlin, the Crater Lake region, the greater Illinois River Valley, Grayback Mountain, Pyramid Peak, the Steve and Sucker Creek drainages, and the California Siskiyous. Weather watchers will delight in observing the cloud changes on a fall day.

When vista-quenched or chased down by the wind, return to Sucker Gap and the Boundary Trail junction. For the loop's conclusion, follow the Boundary Trail to Tannen Lake. The trail briefly travels the ridge above the shelter and its neighboring meadows, before drifting into a conifer forest.

At 11.5 miles, the trail segment forming the abbreviated loop joins the Boundary Trail. The Boundary Trail now begins its rising-dipping course along the ridges, passing low oak bushes, manzanita, tanoak, and conifer. The trail trades views of Pyramid Peak for Tannen Mountain.

At 13 miles, the trail branches. Taking a right leads to Tannen Lake and the conclusion of the loop, retracing the introductory 3 miles of this trail description. The Boundary Trail continues straight, ascending and looping behind Tannen Mountain.

45 CAVE CREEK TO BIG TREE LOOP

Distance: 8.9 miles round trip
Elevation Change: 2600 feet
Difficulty: Strenuous
Maps: USGS Oregon Caves; USFS Siskiyou National Forest, Oregon Caves National Monument brochure
Water: Available at Chalet
Season: Spring through fall
For More Information: Oregon Caves National Monument

It was more than 100 years ago that Elijah Davidson first discovered the caves now known as Oregon Caves, formerly Josephine Caves (named for the county). Yet the above-ground offerings of this park remain undiscovered.

This small park sports a quality trail system, interlocking with major trail systems of the region. The nature trails identify the major forest plants and introduce the above-ground features that contributed to the formation of the underground marble mystery.

While the area geology is the drawing card of the park, a long-time resident, too, commands respect and regard. “Big Tree,” as it is known, is a star by any standard. The Douglas fir measures 41 feet 3 inches in circumference and boasts a diameter of 13 feet 1 inch and a height of 160 feet. The tree is an estimated 1200 to 1500 years old, one of the oldest in Oregon.

Cave Junction opens the door to the above- and below-ground offerings of the monument. From the intersection of U.S. 199 and Oregon 46 in Cave Junction, take Oregon 46 east, following the signs to Oregon Caves National Monument. In 15.3 miles, a right turn leads to Cave Creek Forest Service Campground. During the off-season, park off to the side of the road at the gate. The Cave

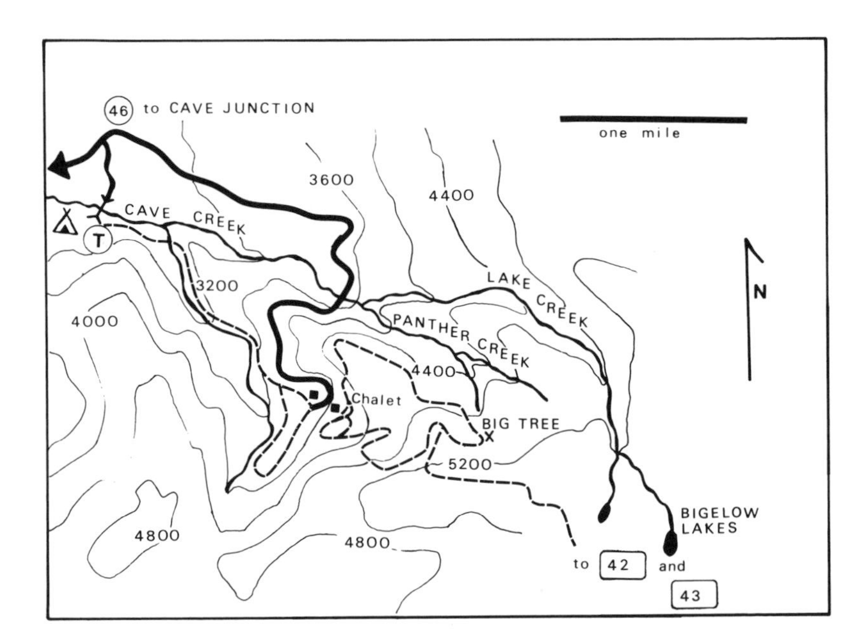

Creek trailhead lies at the end of the campground's one-way loop. The trail is marked.

The Cave Creek Trail begins along the south bank of the waters that give the trail its name. Tanoak, rhododendron, young cedar, and fir line the trail. Salal, Oregon grape, bracken fern, and moss generate swells of green below outspread branches.

The trail begins with a couple of quick switchbacks, then settles into its steady ascent, offering frequent overviews of Cave Creek. The end of May and early June find the dogwood and rhododendron in bloom.

At .3 mile, the trail skirts a clearcut. The blackened earth of the 1987 slash burn will soon depart, but the open skyline will long remain. Where the trail splits, take the lower branch following the creek. The upper branch is the border for the cut.

In a short distance, the trail leaves the burn and crosses the creek. Horsetail reeds, maidenhair ferns, and other water-loving plants thrive creekside.

Viewing the south slope from here, one discovers a living journal of logging activity. Clearcuts, second-growth forests, newly replanted slopes, and old-growth stands that promise to be the next cut boldly greet the eye.

For the next mile, the trail climbs to Oregon Caves National Monument and the junction with No Name Loop. Taking a left on No Name Loop, the trail climbs to the Chateau in .3 mile. Vanilla leaf and bleeding hearts lend their delicate blooms to the forest floor. Where the trail exits at the parking area, a left leads to the Chalet and Big Tree Loop.

To tour Big Tree Loop in a clockwise direction, take a left. The trail climbs the slope above the Chateau and Chalet, through a fir–live oak woodland. There are a few showings of Oregon grape and snowberry among the patchy groundcover. The trail begins paved and eventually returns to forest trail. Benches along the way encourage a lengthier study of the area's natural offerings.

With the ascent of the slope comes the introduction of madrone and manzanita into the forest mix. At 2.6 miles, there's a short spur to a water catchment, and at 2.7 miles the trail enters Siskiyou National Forest. The forest character again changes, returning to tall forest and a varied understory of vanilla leaf, Oregon grape, rhododendron, wild rose, and Indian pipe or corpse plant.

A towering cedar greets the hiker as the trail returns to Oregon Caves National Monument. Big Tree awaits at 3.7 miles. Although a sign precedes this giant, it requires no introduction. Its girth speaks of its longevity and reigning presence in the forest.

Cave entrance, Oregon Caves National Monument

Continuing on the trail, at 4.1 miles the hiker comes to a junction. The trail charging uphill to the left is the Lake Mountain Trail with such destinations as Mt. Elijah (named for the discoverer of the caves), Lake Mountain, and Bigelow Lakes, Hikes 42 and 43. The remainder of the loop lies downhill to the right.

Closing the loop, the trail journeys through a meadow of thigh-high cow parsnip, false hellebore, Indian paintbrush, and asters. The colorations of fall touch the meadow early in the season. At 5.4 miles, the trail meets with the Cliff Nature Trail (a .75-mile loop). Either direction returns to the Chalet.

For the trail's continuance, pass back through the Chalet archway and cross the guest parking lot. At 5.9 miles, No Name Loop begins to the left. The trail starts out on a level course through Douglas fir, madrone, tanoak, and wild rose. The forest floor is relatively open. Cave Creek gurgles in the backdrop.

At 6.4 miles, a spur departs the trail to the left, halting at Cave Creek in 50 yards. A second spur departing the trail likewise ends at the creek. At 6.9 miles, the hiker arrives at the Cave Creek Trail junction.

Return to the vehicle via the Cave Creek Trail, for a round-trip distance of 8.9 miles.

46 BABYFOOT LAKE-CHETCO RIVER LOOP

Distance: 26.8 miles
Elevation Change: 3500 feet
Difficulty: Strenuous
Maps: USGS Pearsoll Peak and Chetco Peak; USFS Kalmiopsis Wilderness/Wild Rogue Wilderness
Water: Maintained safe water sources indicated on the Kalmiopsis Wilderness map (purification recommended); carry extra water as not all sites are dependable
Season: Late spring to early fall
For More Information: Illinois Valley Ranger District

The Kalmiopsis Wilderness is a genuine treasure cache of plants. Several rare and endangered plant species raise their heads here and nowhere else. One of these wonders, *Kalmiopsis leachiana,* a pre-Ice Age member of the heath family, gives the area its name.

The climate of the Kalmiopsis Wilderness produces an unri-

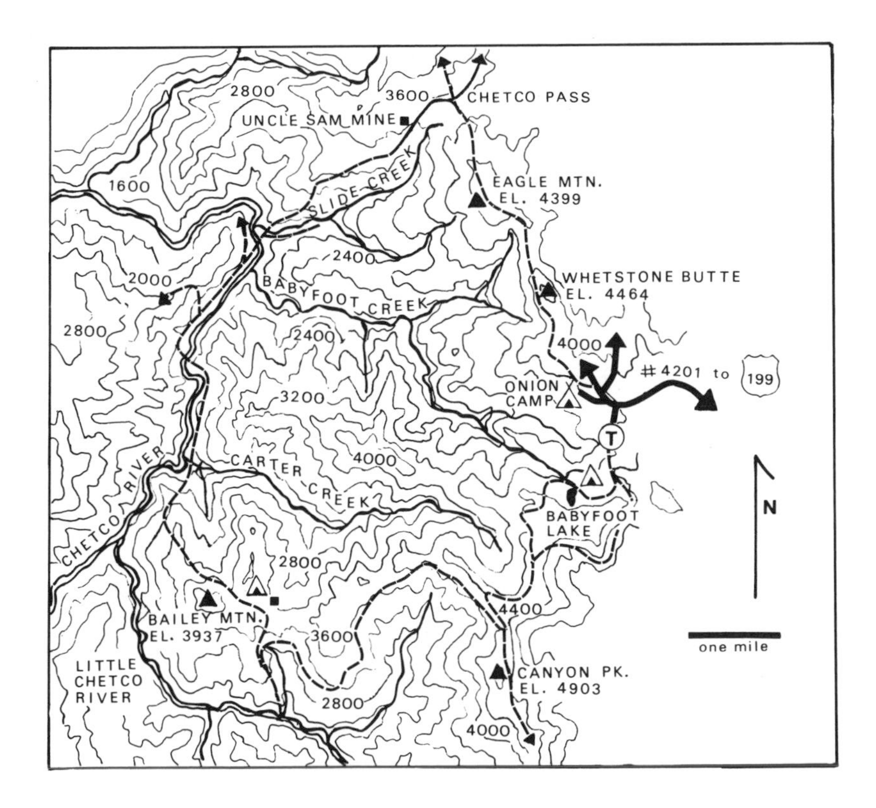

valed transition forest with madrone, tanoak, myrtle, chinquapin, dogwood, azalea, kalmiopsis, rhododendron, weeping spruce, Douglas fir, and Port Orford cedar.

But the featured attraction of this wilderness trail remains Chetco River Canyon with its narrow gorge, steep walls, and deep indigo pools—serene and beckoning. The scenic qualities of this river won it Wild and Scenic River designation in 1988. Two river crossings are required on the loop, but the sight and song of the river alone would tempt the hiker to these waters.

Many hikers declare the trail overlooking the Chetco River Canyon to reign among the most beautiful ever toured. Add to this the exceptional wilderness vistas, a human history of abandoned gold and chromium mines, and the pristine shore and quiet waters of Babyfoot Lake, and this loop is a bona fide winner.

To reach the Babyfoot Lake trailhead from Grants Pass, take U.S. 199 south to 3.7 miles south of Selma, then turn west (right) on Eight Dollar Road where there's a sign for the Kalmiopsis Wilderness. In 1 mile, the road becomes Forest SR 4201 and the surface soon turns into gravel. In 9.5 miles from the U.S. 199 turnoff, bear left for the Kalmiopsis Wilderness, and in another 4.7 miles bear left again to the Babyfoot Lake trailhead. Trailhead parking is in .7 mile.

A forest of Douglas and grand fir, Port Orford cedar, and weeping spruce welcomes the hiker. The groundcover ranges from Oregon grape to succulents. Soon, the hiker arrives at the split-off for the Canyon Peak Trail. For a hiking alternative, this trail bypasses Babyfoot Lake but later rejoins the loop.

Taking the path to Babyfoot Lake, the hiker discovers a drier plant community introduced by the southern exposure. A rocky overlook affords early views of the wilderness. Penstemon and imperial lewisia ornament the outpost.

Babyfoot Lake, centerpiece of Babyfoot Lake Botanical Area, lies ahead at 1.4 miles. It is here that the hiker enters the Kalmiopsis Wilderness. The emerald waters ringed by a rich conifer forest invite the unburdening of a backpack. Campsites are located on the northwest and south sides of the lake.

The trail crosses over Babyfoot Creek, at the northwest end of the lake. From here, the trail climbs to a jeep road. Take a left for the loop. Jeep roads are frequently utilized in the Kalmiopsis trail system. At the upcoming road juncture, continue straight ahead. The mixed conifer forest provides patchy shade.

An old mining set-up rests trailside. Abandoned operations and a few active claims riddle the wilderness. At 3.5 miles, Canyon Peak Trail (mentioned earlier) meets up with the road.

Canyon Peak comes into view just prior to reaching the Little Chetco–Bailey Mountain trail junction at 5 miles. There's a large campsite up the hill to the left. The trail leaving the camp goes to Canyon Peak in 1.1 miles. The final .3-mile scamper to the summit requires pushing through the brush. The site of a former lookout, Canyon Peak offers 360-degree viewing of the wilderness.

Following the road to Bailey Mountain, the hiker soon comes to a fork and can take either branch. Downhill leads to a water tank. The more even course bypasses a mining claim. Granite and serpentine rocks toss back the sunlight as the trail pulls into the open. In .1 mile, the forks merge.

At the next junction, a right leads to Bailey Mountain, Bailey Cabin, and continuation of the loop; a left leads to Emlly Cabin and the Little Chetco River.

The loop trail mounts a ridge and circles left. Kalmiopsis, azalea, and iris color the descent to Bailey Cabin. Early June finds the wildflower showcase in full display.

At 8.9 miles, Bailey Cabin rests amid a woodland meadow. Excellent campsites are secluded in the trees. Along the thin ribbon of creek, pitcher plants abound. The trail to Bailey Mountain heads uphill to the left of the cabin. Dogwoods overhang the trail.

Babyfoot Lake-Chetco River Loop

In a short distance, the Emlly Cabin Trail enters from the left, and in another 100 yards there's a rocky outpost from which to watch the sunrise.

After the trail crosses the Bailey Mountain saddle, it plunges into a dazzling display of rhododendron, kalmiopsis, azalea, and bear grass. The trail then climbs, passing Sowell and Bumby springs.

From 11.1 to 12.4 miles, steep, fast switchbacks carry the hiker down to the Carter Creek–Chetco River confluence. During the descent, Carter Creek Falls can be spied. The noise of the falls announces its presence.

There are campsites on the bench above Carter Creek. Here, poison oak rears its head, as it does alongside the creek. A tree bridge simplifies the creek crossing. From here, the trail climbs into a Douglas fir–myrtle–tanoak woodland.

At 13.4 miles, the trail passes a window to Chetco River Canyon, but then pulls away briefly. When the trail again returns, it traces a narrow ledge above the river for .3 mile of unrivaled beauty. The narrow gorge, tumbling waters, and frequent deep pools create quite a sensation. Steps slow, where normally they would quicken on the sun-baked ledge.

Approaching the point for the river crossing, the trail descends to Blakes Bar and strikes out across the rocky shoreline to the right. The Chetco requires a wet crossing. Sneakers earn their transport for the tenderfoot. Nearby swimming holes delay the return to the trail.

Springtime flooding may prohibit or complicate the crossing. Early-season hikers should contact the Illinois Valley Ranger District to obtain current river conditions.

From the river, the trail climbs to a jeep road. Take a right and one more right at 15.9 miles to reach the second river crossing. Tanoak, dogwood, madrone, and poison oak line the road. Alligator lizards scurry into the vegetation tangle as the approaching boot threatens.

On the opposite shore, follow the road up the slope. Where it forks go downhill to Slide Creek, campsites, and the continuation of the loop. Going right leads to additional campsites and a side excursion to the creek.

As the road climbs from Slide Creek, it is shaded by tall tanoak, madrone, and Douglas fir. The vegetation later changes to manzanita and small pine. At 18.4 miles, the trail passes a wilderness-entry registration point with a trailhead strictly for four-wheel-drives.

From the area of the gate, views of Chetco River Canyon, Whetstone Butte, and Eagle Mountain dominate. To continue the loop, follow the main road left, uphill from the trailhead parking area. In less than a mile, the trail passes Uncle Sam Mine.

The next landmark is a rusted steam shovel. The nearby creek supports a field of pitcher plants that draw the photo enthusiast and naturalist. At 21.6 miles, the hiker arrives at a four-way junction with trails to the Illinois River, Pearsoll Peak, the Chetco River, and Whetstone Butte/Onion Camp. Taking a right toward Whetstone Butte and Onion Camp leads to the close of the loop.

On the open ridge, twisted, runted trees dot the red-colored rock. Views of Pearsoll Peak Lookout and the Chetco River Valley detain the hiker. Scars from World War II mining activity blaze the arid forested slopes. In .2 mile, the trail to Whetstone Butte and Onion Camp departs to the left.

In 1.5 miles, the hiker arrives at the top of Eagle Mountain. Best views are obtained off the trail to the right on a rocky outcrop.

After crossing the Eagle Mountain–Whetstone Butte Saddle, the trail climbs but does not mount Whetstone Butte. However, where the trail leaves the butte to tour the ridge, at 24.3 miles, it's an easy cross-country jaunt to the summit.

From the ridge, it's a pleasant descent through young forest to the Onion Camp trailhead (25.5 miles). Bright-red snow plants puncture the needle layer. From trailhead parking, take a right on the road, pass through the gate, and continue straight. At 26.1 miles, take a right onto Forest SR 4201.140 for the Babyfoot Lake trailhead, returning to the vehicle at 26.8 miles.

47 BUCKSKIN PEAK-ROUGH & READY LAKES LOOP

Distance: 22.6 miles
Elevation Change: 2000 feet
Difficulty: Strenuous
Maps: USGS Chetco Peak; USFS Kalmiopsis Wilderness/Wild Rogue Wilderness
Water: Maintained safe water sources indicated on Kalmiopsis Wilderness map (purification recommended); carry extra water, as not all sources are dependable
Season: Late spring to early fall
For More Information: Illinois Valley Ranger District

Protected since 1946, this 180,000-acre wilderness is noted for its rugged terrain and rare botanics. As a tribute to its botanical significance, the area carries the name of *Kalmiopsis leachiana,* an ancient member of the heath family and just one of the rare plant species found here. An estimated 2000 flowering plants dot the wilderness landscape.

The loop dips into the southeast corner of the wilderness, providing intriguing glimpses of the variety of the Kalmiopsis plant complex. Variations in terrain, temperature, and moisture produce microclimates that draw together such unlikely neighbors as the chinquapin and the bigleaf maple.

Touring the ridgeline, the hiker is treated to views of the Baldface Creek drainage, Doe Gap, Chetco Peak, and the Pacific Ocean. Boulder jumbles and rocky domes provide the vantage points.

Shaped like a giant elk track, Rough & Ready Lakes invites a steep, cross-country descent. Cedars, azaleas, silver snags, grassy benches, and time-etched boulders accent the shallow waters and add to the tranquility of the retreat.

To reach this loop trail from Cave Junction, go south on U.S. 199 for 7.1 miles to O'Brien, turning west onto Lone Mountain Road. In 2.1 miles, the road changes to Forest SR 4402. Remain on Forest SR 4402, taking a right at the junction in another 6.8 miles. Go another 4 miles, then go straight uphill on Forest SR 4402.112. The road is marked "Limited Maintenance, Not Recommended for Low-Clearance Vehicles." Continue on 4402.112. The Biscuit Hill trailhead (exit point of loop) is in 2.9 miles, the Buckskin Peak trailhead in 4.6 miles.

From the Buckskin Peak trailhead, a retired section of Forest SR 4402.112 forms the trail to Doe Gap. Tanoak, rhododendron, chinquapin, and Douglas fir make up the forest mix. At the trail junction in Frantz Meadow, the Frantz Meadow Trail departs to the west and rapidly descends to Baldface Creek. The main trail continues touring the meadow.

As the trail follows the ridge, rock outcrops and domelands punctuate the landscape. Wind-sculpted pine, manzanita, tanoak,

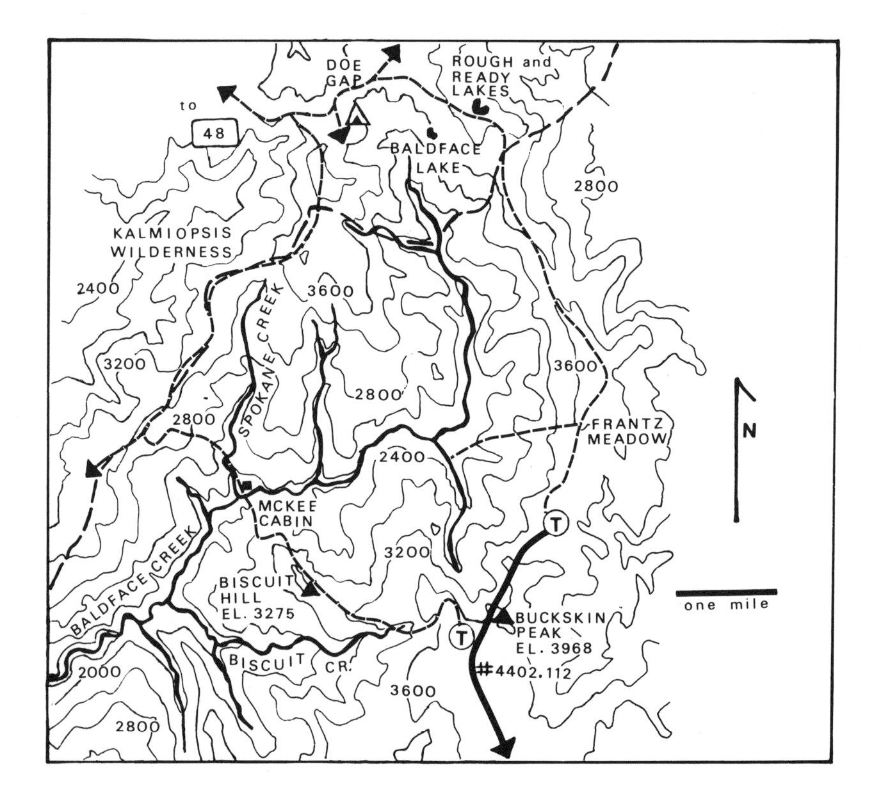

Shelter along the Buckskin Peak-Rough & Ready Lakes Loop

and small myrtle intersperse the rocks. Views of Doe Gap, the Baldface Creek drainage, and Chetco Peak hold the visitor.

Just before entering the Kalmiopsis Wilderness (5.3 miles), the trail flattens out. Venturing off-trail to the east, the hiker finds a view of Rough & Ready Lakes in the basin below.

Visiting the lakes (actually one lake) calls for a steep, rugged cross-country trek downhill. Be alert for wasp nests and use extra care when descending with a full pack. Campsites cleared of rock occupy the southeast side of the lake.

The lake provides a tranquil setting at which to pass the afternoon or set up camp. Its shallow waters percolate with an active population of newts. Towering cedars and fragrant azaleas complement the shoreline.

Forgoing the lake detour, at 6 miles the main trail drops below the ridgeline. The now-collapsed slope has transformed this one-time road into a properly narrow trail. In less than a mile, the trail opens up, offering views to the north of the Chetco River drainage and Hawks Rest. The rush of Baldface Creek replaces the previous loud silence.

At Doe Gap, there's a five-way trail junction. Going downhill to the left leads to a spring and Limber Camp in .4 mile. The completion of the loop lies ahead and to the right on the North Fork Smith River Trail.

As the trail rounds the peak, the rhododendron and azalea of springtime splash the slopes with color. Here, too, the rare Brewer (or weeping) spruce makes an appearance, and openings in the forest provide overviews of the Chetco River Valley. Together, these attractions make this one of the most pleasing stretches of the trail.

At 8.1 miles, the trail again reaches a junction. For the loop, take a sharp V-turn, back up the hill to the left, continuing on the North Fork Smith River Trail. Ground juniper, chinquapin, bear grass, and small pines dress the peak. At the top, take a right on Smith River Way to tour the wilderness boundary.

At the trail junction at 13.9 miles, a left onto the Baldface Trail continues the loop. Following a steep descent, the trail tours a lush, spring-fed grove of fir and pine. Sword and bracken ferns pour over the landscape.

Dry open forest replaces this wet profusion. At 15.3 miles, the trail descends deeper into the tanoak–madrone forest. Here, occasional showings of poison oak dip into the trail, but mostly this evildoer confines itself to the trail fringes.

In a half mile, the hiker encounters the first of several mining ruins. Mining is part of the Kalmiopsis legacy, what with the gold rush of the 1850s and the chrome mines of World War II.

The sparkling threads of Spokane and Baldface creeks grace this area. Both require wading in the spring, but Spokane may allow a dry crossing later in the hiking season.

The fording site for Baldface Creek lies just beyond McKee Cabin, at the prominent cedar. The trail segment that extends beyond the cabin leads to some prized campsites, secluded in the forest.

On the opposite bank, the trail mounts a rocky bar, then heads up a small landslide. Before leaving Baldface Creek, fill the water containers (purification recommended). Biscuit Creek is an unreliable water source, and there's a hot, dusty climb ahead.

Briefly, the trail travels the elevated bank, passing through the hemlock–cedar–fir forest. Myrtle, black huckleberry, and sword and bracken ferns contribute to a rich understory. Departing the streamside abundance, the trail marches up a steep rocky ravine, entering a dense tanoak–fir woodland. An open pine–fir forest later replaces this woodland.

Where a rusting ore wagon rests trailside, the trail begins crisscrossing a one-time wagon road which charges straight up the hill. In this case, the trail offers the more moderate grade.

At 18 miles, the trail delivers an ideal resting site, shaded by the spreading arms of a pine. A grassy carpet and boulder seating await the footsore. Here, one secures views of the loop, Chetco Peak, and the Pacific Ocean.

As the trail tops Biscuit Hill, it merges with the old wagon road. The trail occasionally grows faint, but remains easy to follow. Low bushes border the final leg of the trail. Segments gouged by erosion confound progress.

At 20.9 miles the trail exits at the Biscuit Hill trailhead. A 1.7-mile journey along Forest SR 4402.112 now stands between hiker and vehicle. A left leads to the Buckskin Peak trailhead.

48 CHETCO LAKE

Distance: 9.6 miles round trip (12.6 miles round-trip distance with Navy Monument side trip)
Elevation Change: 300 feet (3100 feet with side trip)
Difficulty: Moderate (strenuous with side trip)
Maps: USGS Chetco Peak; USFS Kalmiopsis Wilderness/Wild Rogue Wilderness
Water: Maintained safe water sources indicated on the Kalmiopsis Wilderness map (purification recommended)
Season: Late spring to early fall
For More Information: Chetco Ranger District

Part of the Chetco Divide Trail, which slices the southern extremity of the Kalmiopsis Wilderness, this trail offers panoramic viewing of the Kalmiopsis, the Chetco River drainage, and neighboring features of the Coast Range. Rounding the flanks of Vulcan Peak and Red Mountain, the trail pursues a rugged, sometimes rocky ridgeline course.

The small, hardy pines and firs which cling to the wind-swept slopes belie the proximity of the coastal redwoods a mere 10 miles away.

Chetco Lake, the destination of this trek, presents an austere face with its open shoreline, isolated stands of cedars and pines,

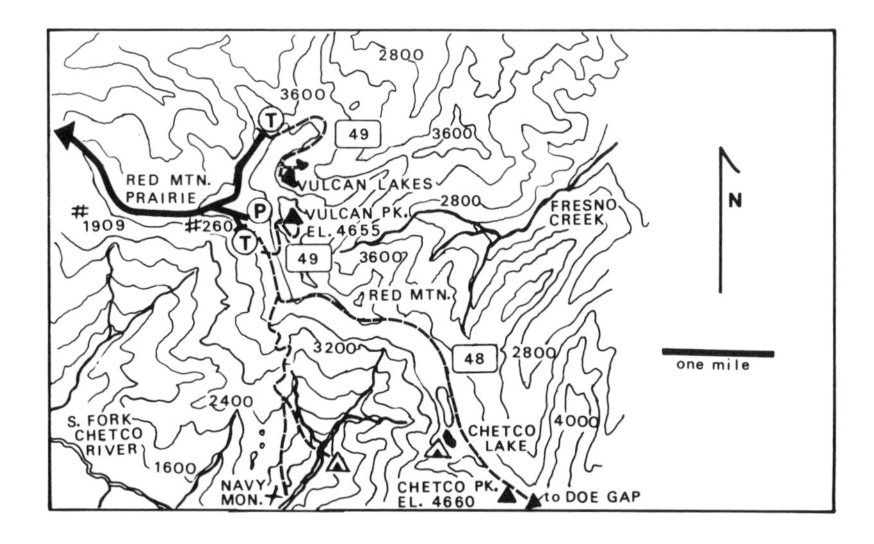

Western azalea on shore of Chetco Lake

and scattered western azaleas. Yet its wind-tossed waters seclude a thriving population of salamanders and newts. In the valley below the lake lies the Navy Monument, a tribute to the men aboard the Navy transport plane that crashed in 1944.

To reach this portion of the Chetco Divide Trail from Brookings, travel east on North Bank Chetco River Road, which later becomes Forest SR 1376. In 13.8 miles the pavement ends, and in another 1.9 miles there's a junction. Take a right onto Forest SR 1909, and stay on it (it takes several turns) for the next 13 miles. A right onto Forest SR 1909.260 leads to the Chetco Divide Trail. Trailhead parking is in .3 mile (at .1 mile, there's a pullout for low-clearance vehicles).

The Chetco Divide Trail starts at the gated road that branches right off Forest SR 1909.260, just prior to trailhead parking.

A reclaimed road, the trail traces the west flank of Vulcan

Peak. Pines and cedars frame its path. Myrtle, tanoak, ground juniper, and dwarfed Oregon grape add texture to the fabric of the slope. Openings in the tree cover offer early views of the Coast Range, Red Mountain Prairie, and the ocean.

The trail begins rocky, but between .3 and 1.3 miles the rocks have been cleared to one side. At 1.3 miles, there's a trail junction. A right leads to the 1944 crash site of a Navy transport plane. It's a steep, 1.5-mile downhill trek to the wreckage site and the monument erected to the crew. Debris from the plane still mars the site.

From the junction, the Divide Trail departs the boundary, pulling east into the wilderness. As the trail rounds the south slope of Vulcan Peak Ridge, views of Red Mountain, Chetco Peak, and the upcoming ridgeline course greet the hiker. Below, to the southwest, the trail to Cottonwood Camp and the Navy Monument cuts a jagged scar through the valley.

The trail next skirts Red Mountain. As the many rock chutes streaking its flank suggest, there's uneven footing ahead. At 2.7 miles, the spur for Van Pelt Spring leaves the right-hand side of the trail. The spring lies downhill about 300 yards.

The ever-present Oregon iris and colorful Indian paintbrush brighten the rugged terrain. Off-trail, several old mines burrow into the sides of the wilderness.

At 3 miles, a small saddle offers a possible campsite, with a nearby trail leading to water. Pitcher plants announce the spring which lies .25 mile down the slope. Beautiful tall cedars and firs intermix with the pines on the bountiful north slope.

From the saddle, the trail narrows, as it draws behind the first knob of the ridge. At 3.6 miles, it pulls out onto the ridge. Wildflowers struggle to gain a stronghold—reds, yellows, pinks, and whites—their fragile stalks bent by the wind.

The trail passes a primitive helicopter pad, then draws behind a second knob. A flat area welcomes the hiker, and western azaleas fan the trail. Their heady perfume saturates the air.

But the open area and the abundance of vegetation misrepresent the nearness of the lake. Not until the hiker has clocked 4.6 miles of trail does Chetco Lake come into view. In .2 mile, a side trail leads to its southeast shore.

This natural lake on the divide is not scenic, but is rich in character. Campsites nestled in the wind-whipped pines and weather-sorry cedars of the southeast shore offer retreat for day visitor and overnighter.

Chetco Lake is a good day-hike destination, but not one that could entertain a weekend backpack. Its camps are, however, well located for hikers continuing on the Divide Trail to Doe Gap and destinations east.

49 VULCAN PEAK AND VULCAN LAKES

Vulcan Peak Trail

Distance: 3 miles round trip
Elevation Change: 900 feet
Difficulty: Moderate
Maps: USGS Chetco Peak; USFS Kalmiopsis Wilderness/Wild Rogue Wilderness
Water: Carry water
Season: Late spring to early fall
For More Information: Chetco Ranger District

See map on page 165.

Vulcan Lake

Distance: 3.6 miles round trip
Elevation Change: 400 feet
Difficulty: Moderate
Maps: USGS Chetco Peak; USFS Kalmiopsis Wilderness/Wild Rogue Wilderness
Water: Vulcan and Little Vulcan lakes (purification recommended)
Season: Late spring to early fall
For More Information: Chetco Ranger District

These two short hikes provide an excellent introduction to the Kalmiopsis Wilderness.

Vulcan Peak (elevation 4655 feet), site of a former lookout, provides lofty overviews of the steep, rugged terrain that is the Kalmiopsis Wilderness. Occupying the southwest border, it also affords views of the Chetco River drainage, the Coast Range, and the fog-filled horizon over the Pacific Ocean. Its red rock face suggests the name "Vulcan"—for the Roman god of fire.

Vulcan and Little Vulcan lakes are classic mountain pools, shimmering fresh at the base of a ridge. Rimmed by evergreens, Vulcan Lake seduces with a mesmerizing charm. Next door, cedars, western azaleas, and a preponderance of pitcher plants punctuate the irregular outline of Little Vulcan Lake. Both lakes welcome a picnic lunch, nature study, and quiet repose.

For these Kalmiopsis Wilderness offerings, travel east from Brookings on North Bank Chetco River Road, which later becomes Forest SR 1376. In 13.8 miles the pavement ends, and in another 1.9 miles there's a junction. Take a right onto Forest SR 1909 and stay on it through several turns for 13 miles.

Taking a right onto Forest SR 1909.260 leads to the Vulcan Peak Trail and trailhead parking in .3 mile (at .1 mile, there's a pullout for low-clearance vehicles). Both Vulcan Peak and Chetco Lake, Hike 48, share this parking area.

A left (staying on 1909) leads to the Vulcan Lake Trail in 1.7 miles. There's a vault toilet at the trailhead for visitor convenience.

Vulcan Peak Trail: This trail begins its ascent up the west-

Overlook of the Kalmiopsis Wilderness

facing slope. Early views of the Coast Range, Red Mountain Prairie, Mt. Emily, and the ocean serve as a preview of the vistas to come. Pine, tanoak, myrtle, and low brush define the rocky trail.

The trail to Vulcan Peak boasts perhaps the most "normal" climb of the Kalmiopsis trail complex. The climb exhibits good design, pace, and grade. Elsewhere in the wilderness, the terrain requires steeply climbing trails. The trailbed to Vulcan Peak, however, is not well formed. Often mirroring the slope, the canted path can cause awkward footing.

At 1 mile, the trail takes a turn, heading east toward the peak. In another .2 mile, the hiker obtains excellent views of the Siskiyou Mountains to the south and the wilderness to the southeast. Charred ruins and melted glass announce the one-time lookout station at the top of Vulcan Peak (1.5 miles). Small, gnarled pines hug the peak.

The summit offers 360-degree viewing. Highlighting the wilderness view are Chetco Peak, Chetco Divide, the Fresno Creek drainage, the Chetco River Valley, Whetstone Butte, Eagle Mountain, and Pearsoll Peak.

While drinking in the surrounding glory, beware that you select a solid perch. Much of the rock on the summit is loose and crumbly.

Return as you came.

Vulcan Lake Trail: As the Peak and Lake trails do not connect, a drive is again in order. Returning to the junction of Forest SR 1909 and 1909.260, hikers travel northeast 1.7 miles on Forest SR 1909 to reach Vulcan Lake trailhead.

Beginning from the roadblock, the trail splits in about 100 feet. Vulcan Lake Trail heads uphill to the right. Johnson Butte and Dry Butte trails go off to the left.

From the junction, Vulcan Lake Trail begins a switching course up the ridge. Pine and cedar define the open-cathedral corridor of the trail. Western azalea, red huckleberry, and bear grass embroider its flanks.

At .6 mile, the trail achieves a rocky, open step. Here, views of the Dry Butte and Box Canyon Creek area ensnare the hiker.

Rounding the ridge, the trail soon makes a no-nonsense descent to the lakes. At 1.25 miles, there's a trail junction, with the Gardner Mine Loop departing to the left. The lakes lie ahead to the right.

The nearly circular, glimmering pool of Vulcan Lake first greets the hiker at 1.5 miles. Scenic lakeside camps await the overnighter. The lake supports a rocky shore.

Pacific newts and salamanders churn the waters near shore. An occasional fish jumping breaks the calm of the water's surface, distorting the reflection of the forested ridge.

From Vulcan Lake, it's a steep descent on rock-studded trail to Little Vulcan Lake. At 1.8 miles, Little Vulcan takes the stage. It's a springtime charmer bordered by cedar stands and western azaleas heavy with pale blooms. Nearby, the crop of bizarre pitcher plants offers an eerie contrast. Tranquility blankets the setting. Both Vulcan and Little Vulcan lakes bid for the hiker's time.

Return as you came.

Along the Redwood Nature Trail

50 REDWOOD NATURE TRAIL #4

Distance: 1-mile loop (self-guided)
Elevation Change: 200 feet
Difficulty: Easy
Maps: USFS Siskiyou National Forest
Water: Elk Creek and the Chetco River
Season: All year
For More Information: Chetco Ranger District

This 1-mile nature trail introduces the visitor to the world's northernmost grove of coastal redwoods. The coastal redwood knows a limited province, growing only in northern California and the southwest corner of Oregon. Residing trailside are monarchs 300 to 800 years old, boasting diameters of 5 to 13 feet.

Interspersed with the redwood is the Douglas fir, the most common conifer in the Pacific Northwest and, in this grove, the skyline rival of the redwood. Rhododendron, which blooms in late spring and early summer, riddles the grove with color and texture. In the fall, it's the evergreen huckleberry, heavy with fruit, that adds to the walk.

The trail guide, complete with descriptions and sketches, introduces the habitat of the redwood grove and the common flora of the Coast Range. The guide also describes the unique features of the coastal redwood that bestow the tree with resilience and longevity.

When touring the trail, tread lightly. A newt may share your path. These sometimes awkward, slow-moving creatures blend well with the needle mat but command an audience once sighted.

To reach the nature trail from the southern coast town of Brookings, take County 784 east, following the signs to Alfred A. Loeb State Park. The park entrance appears on the right in 8 miles. The trailhead turnout lies .5 mile beyond that. The turnout is on the left; the Chetco River is on the right.

Trailhead parking can accommodate two vehicles. Nearby turnouts on County 784 accommodate additional vehicles. A picnic table and vault toilet are provided for visitor convenience.

The trailhead is located at the far end of the picnic area, where trail brochures are generally available. On the bank below, the hiker will note some equipment, actually part of a small fish hatchery. Posted signs warn visitors against trespassing.

For a short distance, the trail follows Elk Creek, then it switches away into the forest proper. The redwood hosts draw the eyes skyward. A point of historical interest along the first section of trail is the rotting remains of a log-cage bear trap.

Gradually, the trail winds its way back to Elk Creek and a bridge crossing, before it charges up the opposite slope. A fallen redwood marks the trail's ascent. Pace off the length of this fallen giant to better appreciate its former height. A denser grove of redwoods, with many family groupings, dominates this slope.

After touring the grove, the trail again works its way down to the creek and out to the road. The hardwoods—Oregon myrtle, red alder, and bigleaf maple—crowd the moist bottomland. The loop, however does not join. The final leg of the journey is a .2-mile trek west along County 784, back to the parking area.

ADDRESSES

Alsea Ranger District
18591 Alsea Highway
Alsea, OR 97324

Bureau of Land Management, Medford
3040 Biddle Road
Medford, OR 97501

Bureau of Land Management, Salem
1717 Fabry Road S.E.
Salem, OR 97302

Cape Perpetua Visitor Center
P. O. Box 274
Yachats, OR 97498

Chetco Ranger District
555 Fifth Street
Brookings, OR 97415

District State Parks Headquarters
Ft. Stevens State Park
Hammond, OR 97121

District State Parks Headquarters
Nehalem Bay State Park
8300R 3rd Street Necarney
Nehalem, OR 97131

District State Parks Headquarters
Sunset Bay State Park
13030 Cape Arago Highway
Coos Bay, OR 97420

Eugene Parks, Recreation and Cultural Services
210 Cheshire Street
Eugene, OR 97401

Galice Ranger District
1465 N.E. 7th Street
P. O. Box 1131 (mailing address)
Grants Pass, OR 97526

Gold Beach Ranger District
1125 S. Ellensburg, Box 7
Gold Beach, OR 97444

Hebo Ranger District
Hebo, OR 97122

Illinois Valley Ranger District
26568 Redwood Highway
Cave Junction, OR 97523

Mapleton Ranger District
Mapleton, OR 97453

Oregon Caves National Monument
Superintendent
19000 Caves Highway
Cave Junction, OR 97523

Oregon Dunes National Recreation Area
855 Highway Avenue
Reedsport, OR 97467

Oregon State Department of Forestry, Forest Grove
801 Gales Creek Road
Forest Grove, OR 97116

Oregon State Department of Forestry, Salem
2600 State Street
Salem, OR 97310

Oregon State Parks and Recreation Division, Salem
525 Trade Street S.E.
Salem, OR 97310

Oregon State University Research Forest
College of Forestry
Corvallis, OR 97331

Powers Ranger District
Powers, OR 97466

Refuge Manager,
Complex Office
William L. Finley National
Wildlife Refuge
26208 Finley Refuge Road
Corvallis, OR 97333

Siskiyou National Forest
Forest Supervisor's Office
200 N.E. Greenfield Road
P. O. Box 440 (mailing address)
Grants Pass, OR 97526

Siuslaw National Forest
Forest Supervisor's Office
4077 Research Way
P. O. Box 1148 (mailing address,
zip code 97339)
Corvallis, OR 97333

Waldport Ranger District
Waldport, OR 97394

INDEX

ABOUT THE AUTHORS

Salem, Oregon residents Rhonda (author) and George (photographer) Ostertag have spent more than a decade hiking extensively in the western states.

Rhonda was born in Montana and transplanted to California, where she took up hiking to escape the city. George left his native Connecticut to study geology in Arizona and to hike and photograph the Desert Southwest. Educational interests took them both to the University of San Diego where they met at the MBA program. A mutual love of the outdoors and a desire to escape from the city eventually led them north to Oregon, and to the remote beauty of the state's "forgotten" mountains.

Rhonda is a freelance writer specializing in travel, outdoor recreation and nature topics. George has participated in several environmental impact studies including the California Desert Bill. Both are involved members of the Wilderness Society, The Nature Conservancy, the National Wildlife Federation, and several other conservation-oriented organizations.

The Ostertags' collaboration in writing and photography has produced articles in *Westways, The Los Angeles Times, Newsday, Backpacker, Trailer Life* and numerous other local and national publications on topics ranging from elephant seals to wildflowers, spelunking and condor-watching.